Rehabilitation in Community Mental Health

H. Richard Lamb and Associates
Foreword by Bertram J. Black

REHABILITATION IN COMMUNITY MENTAL HEALTH

 Jossey-Bass Inc., Publishers

San Francisco · Washington · London · 1971

The Jossey-Bass
Behavioral Science Series

General Editors

WILLIAM E. HENRY
University of Chicago

NEVITT SANFORD
Wright Institute, Berkeley

Foreword

In this country rehabilitation of the mentally ill, as a formal process, is not more than two decades old. It began with tentative reachings out to mental hospitals by community services for the physically disabled, moved strongly into the hospitals themselves, and has now begun to evolve programs of its own in the communities in which the mentally handicapped and disabled live. This almost full circle has been a difficult one. It was hard at the beginning to interest mental hospitals in rehabilitation; it was difficult, too, to convince many hospitals to develop rehabilitation services. It took years to arouse interest in rehabilitation facilities for the mentally ill outside of the hospitals, and outside is where rehabilitation belongs.

Signs have been pointing to the community as the optimum environment for rehabilitation all the time. At one of the first planning meetings about psychiatric rehabilitation, in the middle 1950's, the late T. P. Rees, the well known British psychiatrist, proposed that doctors be moved out of the mental hospitals so that the patients would follow. Few mental hospital directors paid heed. Then both the National Institute of Mental Health and the Federal Vocational Rehabilitation Administration offered support to demonstration projects in rehabilitation, both in hospitals and outside of them. The landmark Community Mental Health Centers Act of 1963 included rehabilitation among the ten elements of a community mental health center program, although not among the "five essentials." As some of us predicted years ago, however, the signs could not be ignored, and today hardly a modern mental health program in this country or abroad does not claim rehabilitation as a prominent modality in its services.

Psychiatric rehabilitation in the community is an idea whose time has come. We have been moving patients ever more swiftly through inpatient services and have devised ingenious alternatives to mental hospitalization: day and night hospitals, day care centers, halfway houses and hostels, crisis intervention teams, and the like. Raising the competency levels of persons with psychiatric disabilities, increasing their functioning capacities, has become the goal of an increasing number of hospitals, clinics, and mental health centers. As we have become accepting of the sad fact that we do not have the methods of "curing" psychoses, we have begun to stress alleviating symptoms and helping patients to live with or to overcome their residual handicaps.

This approach raises the question of what is treatment and what is rehabilitation. I am pleased that this book avoids the semantic trap of trying to answer this question. Perhaps all treatment of mental illness—medical, psychological, or social—is rehabilitation. And perhaps the rehabilitation process is in reality a form of treatment. In terms of the health delivery system the answer is immaterial. What is important, as is stressed in this book, is that a wide array of programs and services makes up the rehabilitation armamentarium. Some of these services are familiar to the mental health professions, but some are highly specialized professional or paraprofessional services more familiar to workers in welfare or education or rehabilitation of the physically handicapped. It is the interplay and integration of all of these resources that makes psychiatric rehabilitation in the community of special importance.

There is also the accumulation of experience that must be heeded. We know now that even the most wonderful programs in the mental hospitals—of rehabilitation orientation and emphasis and with all the specializations and facilities available—do little more than speed up the return of patients to the community. They do not keep patients out of the hospitals. On the other hand, demonstration after demonstration has shown that community rehabilitation services can decrease or at least shorten subsequent hospital stay.

To a great extent, Rees's wish has come to pass. With the growth of community mental health services, psychiatrists have moved into the community and the patients with them. Rehabilitation programs, as described in this book, will help to keep them there.

New York
September 1971

BERTRAM J. BLACK
Professor of Psychiatry
    (Rehabilitation),
Albert Einstein College of Medicine
Director, Mental Health Rehabilitation Services,
Bronx State Hospital
Deputy Director for Rehabilitation Planning,
New York State Department of Mental Hygiene

Preface

Rehabilitation in Community Mental Health grew out of a series of brainstorming sessions by the five authors. It gains unity in that the authors generally share a point of view about rehabilitation in community mental health and subscribe to a set of basic concepts. These are set forth and discussed in some detail in the first chapter. Building on these concepts, the authors then take the reader through the philosophy and practical aspects of rehabilitation counseling, the sheltered workshop, and the various kinds of sheltered work placements, therapeutic housing, and social rehabilitation. The last chapter turns to the evaluation of rehabilitation programs, explores some of the difficulties, and emphasizes the importance of objective assessment.

It is the authors' purpose in particular to acquaint the reader with various aspects of the rehabilitation of persons with emotional problems and to facilitate his appropriate use of the diversity of rehabilitation services. This book is for those workers in rehabilitation who wish to apply their skills to the field of mental health and for those workers in community mental health who wish to increase their participation in the rehabilitation of their clients. It is designed for both students and practitioners.

We express appreciation for the invaluable editorial assistance of Arlene Reiff (psychiatric social worker) and Doris Lamb (psychiatrist and wife of the editor).

San Mateo, California   H. RICHARD LAMB
September 1971

Contents

xv

Contents

Authors

VICTOR GOERTZEL is a research psychologist with the San Mateo County (California) Mental Health Services.

H. RICHARD LAMB is chief of psychiatric rehabilitation services with the San Mateo County (California) Mental Health Services.

CECILE MACKOTA is vocational services supervisor for the San Mateo County (California) Mental Health Services.

CHARLES RICHMOND is the executive director of Mental Health Recovery, Inc., in San Mateo County, California.

ISADORE SALKIND is director of the Rehabilitation Workshop Administration Training Program at the University of San Francisco.

Rehabilitation in Community Mental Health

CHAPTER 1

Essential Concepts

H. Richard Lamb

Rehabilitation of the psychiatric patient is a complex specialty. We believe this specialty is most effective when vocational and social rehabilitation and other mental health treatment are combined in a coordinated effort (Lamb, 1971). Although professionals in each of these fields work within the context of their own disciplines, there are, in the opinion of the authors of this book, a number of basic concepts which underlie the rehabilitation process.

Rehabilitation of psychiatric patients may take place in a hospital or in the community. Our conviction is that, whenever possible, the rehabilitation process should be conducted in the community. A person should be in a hospital because he needs hospitalization, not solely in order to participate in a hospital rehabilitation program. Rehabilitation, to be most effective, should begin as early as possible, but the patient should be discharged to a community program as soon as he is ready.

Regardless of the amount of psychopathology in evidence, there is always an intact portion of the ego to which the rehabilitation effort must be directed. The goal is to expand the remaining well part of the person instead of to remove or cure pathology. The focus here is on the healthy part of the personality, the strengths of the person. Even though pathology is left alone, when the healthy part of the personality is expanded, the person becomes better able to function (Beard, Goertzel, and Pearce, 1958). Rehabilitation focuses on reality factors, rather than on intrapsychic phenomena, and on changing behavior rather than on changing basic character structure.

The concept of ego strength is crucial. For instance, evaluating a client's vocational and intellectual capacity, apart from his emotional strengths and weaknesses, provides only an incomplete picture of what that client can do vocationally. This seems almost self-evident and yet, in our experience with our own and other agencies, we find that failure to take into account a client's emotional capacity is a leading cause of unsuccessful vocational plans. An example is cited in Chapter Two of a schizophrenic graduate engineer who could not be stabilized either psychiatrically or vocationally until he lowered his goals and took a permanent job at the post office.

Involved in this concept of ego strength is the ability to withstand pressure and cope with the usual crises of life, without cracking under the strain, and fleeing from the situation through an overt mental illness, either psychotic or neurotic, or through a psychosomatic condition such as a peptic ulcer, or by having a serious "accident" that removes him from the situation, or by getting drunk and forcing the employer to fire him. Additionally, ego strength involves the ability to be independent. Most of us take for granted our ability to be in competitive employment, to live independently in the community, and to take on the responsibilities of a family. For a person with limited ego strength, however, any one or all of these activities may produce overwhelming pressures. If a crisis arises, a person who lacks ego strength needs immediate help to deal with it. If he has interested and competent friends and relatives to whom he can turn, he may be able to weather such crises. Even then, he may also need the availability of immediate help from such persons as his psychotherapist, vocational counselor, halfway house manager or the psychiatrist on call in a hospital emergency room. The ready availability of crisis intervention personnel is necessary to sustain most long-term mentally ill persons in the community.

In the area of work, rehabilitation emphasizes behavioral problems and personality adjustment on the job, not just aptitude, skills, and training. Neff (1968), in describing the worker role, points out that job aptitude and skills are only part of the essential requirements.

[The individual who can meet these requirements] is able to distinguish the work place both from home and the playing field and adjust his behavior accordingly. He is able to leave his home to go to work without falling apart in the process. He is capable, within limits, of looking and behaving like other members of his work group. He can "turn on" all those behaviors appropriate to work and "turn off" all those affects and needs which are mobilized and gratified by other settings. He can regulate his life by the clock, to the degree that the job requires. He can permit himself to be supervised by strangers, without being rendered so angry by supervision that he cannot function or so servile that he loses all initiative. He can relate to his fellow workers in ways that they deem acceptable.

For a mentally ill person, the worker role can present an imposing set of demands.

But recognizing that a person has limited ego strength does not mean that we expect nothing of him. Central to rehabilitation is the concept of maintaining high expectations so that people strive to reach their full social and vocational potential, even though this potential may be limited. Simply gratifying dependency needs is not rehabilitation. The rehabilitation staff must make it clear that clients are expected to make maximum use of their rehabilitation programs

3

and to function at their full capacities. As Freeman and Simmons (1963) say, "It is crucial that we maintain as high expectations of social participation and work performance as is realistic because low expectations simply support the socially deviant performance and reinforce the patient's failure to perform in ways defined by the role expectations of the larger society."

A high expectations approach makes it all the more important to evaluate each individual carefully to gain an accurate estimate of his potential and his limitations. The goal should be to expect clients to fully utilize their strengths, but we must not expect too much too fast. Programs should allow a plan to be tailored to the needs of each individual. If a rehabilitation center offers a comprehensive social and vocational program, the staff must not expect every client to participate in every phase. Some persons may not be ready, others may be unwilling, to involve themselves in one phase or another. If the center is too rigid, many clients may be excluded who could otherwise be helped. The approach we advocate is high expectations with flexibility.

Befouling the Rehabilitation Process

Vocational rehabilitation agencies have, in recent years, increasingly directed their efforts toward the mentally ill; in fact this was the largest single disability group reported as rehabilitated in 1970. But all too often vocational rehabilitation agencies have a high rate of failure with ex-mental patients because they overlook the need for supportive services such as halfway houses or perhaps, as mentioned later, a sheltered subsociety. Vocational rehabilitation, no matter how innovative and well conceived, cannot take place in a vacuum, especially for chronic mentally ill patients. Because the vocational program occupies only a fraction of a client's waking hours, leisure activities and housing needs are also necessary ingredients for a successful rehabilitation plan.

Large numbers of ex-mental patients who could benefit from rehabilitation services do not receive them (Cohen and Orzech, 1970). Too many rehabilitation agencies play the numbers game.

4

In order to show success, they select only those applicants who can be placed in competitive employment after only a relatively brief period of rehabilitation. Both criteria—suitability for competitive employment and a need for only brief services—often are unrealistic for chronic and severely mentally ill persons as compared with other disabled groups.

Overly-enthusiastic efforts at rehabilitation are sometimes made where it is inappropriate, as part of a ritualistic effort to uphold our cherished values of independence and productivity. We often try to justify sheltered facilities by saying they are designed to lead to independence and economic self-sufficiency for all clients. For instance, the public, and indeed the agency itself, often need to perceive the sheltered workshop (see Chapter 3) as a transitional facility for all its clients when, in fact, many expatients are unable to move beyond them to competitive employment. Clients who after lengthy evaluation clearly need a program of terminal (permanent) sheltered workshop or an activity center or both may be retained in a transitional program with the stated goal of competitive employment. This can be painful for both the clients and the agency.

The Marginal Person in the Community

There is now a strong trend to move patients, including those who have been hospitalized for many years, out of mental hospitals and into the community. One reason is that the community mental health movement has developed expertise in handling psychosocial problems without removing the problem person from the community. Another reason is that society has exhibited increased tolerance of dependency, as evidenced by the public concern with social welfare. Welfare benefits, aid to the disabled, and sheltered living, vocational, and social facilities in the community are more readily available than they were previously. Thus, many persons after leaving hospitals find themselves in the equivalent of a sheltered subsociety. In some cases this is an active, stimulating environment, as in Fairweather's project (1969). He had concluded that most long-term hospitalized patients are not able to live independently in the community and engage in competitive employment. He therefore carefully set up a sheltered subsociety in the community in which expatients lived together and operated their own janitorial service. In this vocational enterprise each man was expected to work not at the normal pace of persons in the community but to his capacity, as in the principle of the sheltered workshop, and he was paid according to his performance. (A more detailed description of Fairweather's program is included in Chapter Five.)

The sheltered subsociety can be either a positive and constructive force toward rehabilitation or a terrible liability. Available to many patients leaving the hospital is a variety of sheltered rehabilitation facilities—such as halfway houses, day treatment centers, and sheltered workshops—in which activity and problem solving are emphasized.

In contrast, many patients find themselves sent to boarding homes or family care homes which, although they are located in the community, often resemble back wards in state hospitals. The atmosphere is depressing, not because of the physical appearance of the boarding home but because of the passivity, isolation, and inactivity of the residents. They lack spontaneity, spend much of their day watching television and relate to boarding home operators as a child does to a parent. In many family care and boarding homes, the residents are kept out of the kitchen and often no responsibility is given to them beyond some attempt at encouraging self-care. Silberstein (1969) describes the situation clearly:

All of the care homes (twenty-two) I visited were operated by women. Husbands, if any, were only peripherally involved in the operation of the homes. Most of the women, prior to becoming caretakers, had jobs in which they provided physical care to sick, aged, or disabled persons. The caretakers were quite maternal, met the physical needs of their guests, and related to them as they would to young children. They expected their residents to be docile recipients of services. Few caretakers delegated any responsibilities to their guests and did not feel these former patients were capable of handling them. However, in several homes, where the caretaker was suddenly hospitalized, the residents had immediately and competently taken over the management of the home until the caretaker returned whereupon they again became docile recipients of services. Patients feared the caretaker's displeasure. Disagreements between the caretaker and residents seldom occurred openly and, when they did, often resulted in the resident's having to leave the home. Caretakers often viewed the expression of anger or annoyance by a resident as an indication of mental illness and would then consult their doctor or social worker for medication for the patient. If the caretaker dealt with disagreements herself, she often did so by either ignoring them or reprimanding the patient as a mother would a young child.

Thus, boarding homes are for the most part so structured that they maximize the state hospital-like atmosphere. Boarding home operators who want a group of quiet, docile, "good" patients are abetted by the monetary reward system of the boarding home, for they are paid by the head rather than rewarded for encouraging rehabilitation efforts on the part of their guests. There are, of course, exceptions. A few boarding home operators actively encourage their guests to use community social and vocational rehabilitation facilities.

We see, then, that the rehabilitation worker must know his community resources. As described in Chapter 6, some halfway houses require that their residents participate in a rehabilitation program. Having a client in a low expectation boarding home can have far different implications than having the same client in a high expectation halfway house (Lamb and Goertzel, 1971).

Olshansky (1968) challenges some assumptions long held in psychiatric rehabilitation. First, there is not, as many have supposed, a clear relationship between work capacity and degree of emotional recovery—that is, the ability to obtain a job and then perform it does not require a certain degree of wellness. Some of the sickest and most disturbed people are able to work, some marginally, some with a high degree of competence. Secondly, it is often

7

assumed that people first have to be socialized before they are able to go to work, that they first have to achieve a high enough level of social skills to get along with other people on some basis of reciprocity. But we have found, like Olshansky, that this is not necessarily the case. Some expatients can act appropriately within a structured work situation where cues are available to guide them but may be immobilized and confused by the lack of structure in a social situation. Others may achieve a high level of social skills but be unable or unwilling to work.

It is all well and good to talk about rehabilitation and maintaining high expectations. But it must be recognized that many persons, including some with a high level of social skills, do not want to find a place in the world of work. Possibly they are fearful of assuming the responsibility and independence inherent in work. If an expatient chooses to be unemployed, our public welfare system ensures that he will be taken care of at a low, but steadily increasing, level. Although a deliberate choice of a role outside of the world of work carries low status, the rehabilitation worker must reconcile himself to the fact that some of his clients will opt out and choose not to be rehabilitated in terms of work.

Labeling and Delabeling

How does a person become labeled as mentally ill? Scheff (1966) presents a point of view from the perspective of sociology which is too often neglected in the discussion of psychiatric patients. First of all, symptoms of mental illness are viewed as violations of social norms. Such behavior as rambling or disorganized speech, unprovoked violent outbursts, delusions, attempts at suicide, bizarre facial grimacing, and extreme anxiety are clearly abnormal by most social standards.

Many such gross violations are not noticed, however, or are ignored or, if noticed, are rationalized as eccentricity. A close look at any neighborhood in any community will reveal large numbers of seriously disturbed persons who have never come to the attention of a psychiatrist. The violation of the social norm in itself, there-

8

fore, does not necessarily cause a person to be labeled as mentally ill. He is labeled, rather, when circumstances bring about public and official recognition of his aberrant behavior—for example, when his family requests that he be committed to a mental hospital. The result? A person stigmatized and labeled as mentally ill.

Scheff points out that labeling of a person as mentally ill is facilitated by stereotyped imagery learned in early childhood and continually reaffirmed, inadvertently, in ordinary social interaction and through the mass media. Thus, when a person's violation of social norms or deviance becomes a public issue, the traditional stereotype of "crazy person" is readily adopted both by those reacting to the deviant and, often, by the deviant himself.

A person completes the process of acquiring the label "mentally ill" when the stereotyped imagery becomes part of his own self-concept and begins to guide his behavior. In a crisis, when the gross violator of social norms is publicly recognized, he is profoundly confused, anxious, and ashamed. The deviant may be highly suggestible and may accept the proferred label of mentally ill as the only way of extricating himself from an intolerable situation. He may prefer being taken to a hospital as crazy to being taken to jail as a shoplifter. Later on, he finds that playing the stereotyped deviant role of being mentally ill gives him such rewards as hospitalization, where he is taken care of, and relief from having to fulfill his normal social and vocational role. Once having been labeled, the "mentally ill person" may find it difficult to divest himself of the label.

Scheff makes an important contribution to understanding labeling, though it should be kept in mind that he exaggerates his position in order to stress his points; he overemphasizes social processes and understresses intrapsychic processes.

Friedson (1965) points out that characteristically the deviant career consists of a progressive narrowing of alternatives until none but the deviant role remains. For example, the more a man becomes known as an exconvict, the fewer options society holds open to him. Moreover, the deviant career is often carried out in facilities such as jails and mental institutions which are segregated

9

from the community at large. When the stigma attached to the deviant role is strong, segregation is extreme, physically as well as socially divorcing the deviant from the everyday community.

Violation of social norms does not always lead to a deviant career. As Scheff points out, symptoms of mental illness are frequently ignored or rationalized. This pattern of inattention, referred to by sociologists as "denial" or "normalization," is used in treating combat neurosis in the armed forces. Few soldiers, labeled mentally ill and sent to psychiatric wards, return to duty. In contrast, when denial is utilized in the treatment a soldier is allowed to have a brief respite from combat a short distance from the combat zone. He is given the message that what happened to him could have happened to anyone under the stress of combat and that it is expected he will be able to return to his unit. Such an approach results in most men returning to duty.

Denial is used similarly in community mental health crisis intervention techniques. The patient is seen for a short time, and the therapist or counselor focuses on strengths rather than pathology. The patient is given the message that he is a functioning member of the community who needs only temporary assistance. The concepts of characterological versus situational are important in this context. Rather than saying to the person that he has a deep-seated intrapsychic problem (characterological), you tell him that his present problem is related to external situational factors under which anyone would have had difficulty. The issue is not whether in fact the mental problem is characterological or situational; usually it's both in varying degrees. What is important is that the person involved not see himself as inherently defective and inferior in a way that sets him apart from society. He must see himself as having strengths in addition to his problems, and he must feel that he has social and vocational alternatives open to him beyond the patient role. Taking a situational point of view can often be a way of helping the patient maintain a positive self-image.

The use of denial is often a crucial factor in the successful adjustment of ex-hospital patients. Thus, having shed his patient identity, the expatient can say that he was physically ill and is now

10

recovered. He can say he "blacked out" and attribute his recovery either to psychiatric treatment or to a spontaneous remission. He can deny that he ever was ill and avoid or guard against the persons and situations which led to his hospitalization. He can claim it was an error or misunderstanding. Or he can see the process as situational, that given the particular set of circumstances in which he found himself, a mental hospitalization would have happened to anyone. But there is more to rehabilitation than the use of denial, especially for chronically and severely ill people. Most severely ill ex-hospital patients also need to remain on medication and participate in a rehabilitation program conducted in a setting where stigma and labeling are minimized. If a person's strengths are emphasized and he is encouraged to live up to his potential, he can make use of rehabilitation facilities and still see himself as a capable, worthwhile person.

Obviously, the use of sheltered facilities involves some element of segregation. The important factors, however, are the role expectations in that setting. A segregated setting need not imply that the person is permanently disabled or that he should spend his life in hospitals or in nonproductive passivity and dependency in the community. Here, the concept of maintaining high expectations plays a crucial role in effective rehabilitation efforts. Mental health professionals must accept the responsibility to encourage and, in some cases, to push clients toward higher levels of social participation and work performance. It should be stressed to client and public alike, that the need for sheltered facilities does not exempt a person from taking his place in society to the full extent of his capabilities.

Our primary aim should be to eliminate the stigma. By accepting a place in an agency or in a sheltered sub-society or rehabilitation agency, the client may well be segregated. However, he need not be stigmatized if he feels accepted by the staff and fellow clients, and is treated with dignity, and feels there is a place for him in society aside from the role of mental patient. The stigma is reduced if he realizes he has strengths which make him "not just a mental patient," but a person who has positive qualities, in addition to whatever emotional problems he may have. Then he is not self-stigmatized nor so readily negatively labeled by others; we have facilitated the process of delabeling.

Here are some of the sociological criteria used to determine whether delabeling has taken place: Is denial (normalization) taking place? What are the role expectations? Does the person see himself primarily as a patient or as a citizen? Is he expected to realize his potential for social and vocational performance in the community? Has stigmatization been reduced to a minimum?

Not all chronic psychiatric patients, or marginal and inept persons in general, need a sheltered subsociety. Goode (1967) has shown that most social institutions find ways to protect the inept without necessarily labeling them as inept or as mentally ill or as anything other than members of the institutions involved. Thus, industry, the military, and governmental agencies find ways to utilize and protect marginal persons who suffer from varying degrees of inadequacy and ineptness. Some industries, particularly large public utilities, have set up sheltered workshops for retraining employees who have become disabled. Generally, the requirements for entering these competitive systems are higher than the requirements for remaining in them. At the time of hiring, a person usually must show promise of productivity and, indeed, he must be able to maintain productivity for some time before the institution feels obligated to find a sheltered position for him within the system. Consequently, many persons whom mental health professionals might consider "psychiatrically disturbed" have found their niche in various institutions. Even though their productivity is sub par, they find support from a large organization, continue to work, and avoid being labeled.

We find it useful to regard the chronic mentally ill person as one category of inept persons. We can summarize much of what has been said in Table 1.

Sociological and Psychological Perspectives

Miller, Dawson, and Barnhouse (1968), in developing a sociopsychological theory of rehabilitation, identify two factors essen-

Table 1. INEPT PERSONS

Status	Persons Stigmatized and Labeled Mentally Ill	Persons Not Stigmatized and Labeled Mentally Ill	
	Segregated	Segregated	Not Segregated
Type of Protection	State hospital	Sheltered sub-societies which maintain high expectations, like that of Fairweather	Protection of the inept in industry and government
Vocational	Sheltered employment in some cases	Sheltered employment	Paid competitive employment (protected)
Living	Hospital	Sheltered facility (halfway house, satellite housing program)—see Chapter 6	Family, alone, sometimes boarding house or residence club

NOTE: This scheme does not include persons who would be considered inept who are living with family or are alone and are dependent on welfare agencies or their families. These persons may or may not be labeled mentally ill.

tial to successful rehabilitation: (1) The ex-hospital patient must have a supporting, accepting reference group. It may be composed of family, friends, or others who are significant to him. Members of this accepting reference group must view him, at least to some degree, as a valuable, functioning member of their group, and he in turn must see himself not as "sick" but as a capable, worthwhile person. (2) He must attain an adequate level of social and economic stability. He must have a place to live and a stable source of income. In short, the former mental patient must be able to say, "I have a place; I am accepted; I am not sick; I am picking up the pieces of my life again." Expatients who are able to find jobs, attain adequate incomes, and perform in socially competent ways are most likely to maintain themselves in the community. Given a certain amount of interpersonal and economic resources and some level of personal socialization, most persons, no matter how "psychiatrically disabled," should be able to remain outside of a state hospital and to participate in the social and family life of their community. If a client cannot find such supports on his own, he must be assisted to acquire them or the rehabilitation process will fail.

Thus far, we have stressed the social aspects of mental illness, for until recently mental illness was defined largely in terms of diagnosis, symptoms, and intrapsychic phenomena, with too little attention given to its social causes and consequences (Maisel, 1967; Scheff, 1966). Understanding the societal reaction to deviant behavior is necessary to understanding both the nature and the course of mental illness. We should not neglect the importance of a person's intrapsychic characteristics, however. Mental illness does exist; it is not exclusively the result of the societal reaction. Because of a lack of ego strength, many people may fall back on emotional disorders such as psychosis, neurosis, psychosomatic disorder, alcoholism, or drug abuse in order to avoid the normal stresses of life. And a long-term hospitalized patient usually is characterized by overwhelming dependency needs in a society where independence is part of one's prized self-image (Wilensky, 1964). Subjective feelings of discomfort may cause such people to ask to be hospitalized. Indeed, the mental hospital can serve as a refuge, a true asylum for people who need to escape from overwhelming pressures. Others, because of their own lack of internal controls, require the increased external controls of the hospital.

In total institutions, such as state mental hospitals, impersonal treatment can strip away a patient's dignity, his individuality and foster regression. Thus the deviant person finds himself locked into a degraded, stigmatized, deviant role (Goffman, 1961; Ludwig and Farrelly, 1966). However, the trend toward milieu therapy and the use of the therapeutic community in mental hospitals and in some prisons has been quite successful in counteracting the process of degradation, stigmatization, and regression that has long characterized the phenomenon of institutionalization (Jones, 1967; Wilmer and Lamb, 1969; Abroms, 1969). Proponents of the therapeutic community and milieu therapy have demonstrated that the social interactions within such community rehabilitation facilities as day treatment centers and halfway houses also can be made therapeutic and instrumental in the work of rehabilitation.

Briefly, as described by Maxwell Jones (1958), the therapeutic community is oriented toward restoring patients to healthy, normal social roles by altering the hospital or institutional structure so that these roles are expected of the patient while he is still in the institution. It is assumed that patients can help in the treatment of other patients and can share in decision-making with the staff. The therapeutic community is committed to the idea that socioenvironmental and interpersonal influences play an important part in the treatment program and is characterized by an atmosphere of intimate, spontaneous face-to-face interactions in which lines of communication are relatively free for both patients and staff. Jones feels that the community must be so designed that group therapy, group activities, and community meetings are essential elements in the propagation of its cultural themes. The therapeutic community, by helping persons in institutions and in community rehabilitation facilities such as social clubs and day treatment centers move away

15

from a degraded, stigmatized role, can be an important factor in the delabeling process.

The Meaning of Work

The importance of work in the rehabilitation of ex-mental patients cannot be overemphasized.

With the evolution of society, achievement has become more and more important as a factor in establishing one's identity. Self-esteem and one's self-image depend in large measure on what one does occupationally and how successful one is in doing it. No longer, as in earlier societies, is one classified primarily by birth, family, and station. For these reasons, any attempt at treatment of the mentally ill and emotionally troubled must, in some way, deal with the issues of occupational choice and vocational satisfaction. Most persons find it difficult to feel themselves a part of society if they are not in the working community. In general, our society disapproves of those who do not work. Most people, consciously or unconsciously, accept society's view and suffer a lowered self-esteem if they do not meet the standards of society. Conversely, the ability to work and to be productive heightens one's self-esteem. The feeling that one is conforming to the norms of society is very much bound up in one's sense of well-being. The contribution of a sense of occupational failure in many cases of depression demonstrates this point [Lamb and Mackota, 1969].

Work serves a primordial function as well. Studies have shown that most men, including those who say that work does nothing for their sense of importance and usefulness, feel that they would nevertheless continue to work in the absence of economic need (Weiss and Kahn, 1959). Less than one-tenth of the men studied report that they would go on working because they enjoy the work itself. As Wilensky (1964) points out, "What the vast majority seem to be trying to say is that they want to remain among the living." The primordial function of work is dramatized by the narrow range of social contact for those squeezed out of the labor market; the aged, the school dropouts, the unemployed, and the underemployed are isolated from the mainstream of community life.

An important concept is that of distinguishing ego-involving jobs from society-maintaining jobs (Havighurst, 1964). An ego-involving job is the organizing force in a person's life. He lives for it, and his life would be empty without it. He does not count his working hours. His job gives him a feeling of being creative, of being of service to people, of being in a prestigious high-status occupation. Ego-involving jobs are positions in which a person can control his job, is free to choose tasks which are of interest to him, and can determine what to do and how to do it. Jobs which are likely to be ego-involving are executive positions in business or government, research, writing, medicine, law, and sometimes skilled crafts.

Society-maintaining jobs, on the other hand, take a far less important place in a person's life and are not a central organizing force for him. A society-maintaining job may require a great deal of skill, but the satisfactions derived from it are likely to be those of association with friends on the job, the money earned, and a pleasant or at least tolerable routine for passing the time. Included in this category are factory jobs, clerical jobs, retail sales work, and most unskilled and semiskilled labor.

Closely tied to the concept of ego-involving and society-maintaining jobs is the problem of work alienation, a condition in which a person feels that his work is meaningless or that it gives him no sense of purpose. Wilensky (1964) approaches this problem by asking how well a man's work role suits his prized self-image— that is, to what extent is the work he does congruent with the kind of person he would like to be and with the kind of person he is at his best. A worker tends to feel alienated in an organizational setting which provides little discretion in pace and schedule or when a tall hierarchy of bosses above him results in low freedom and high pressure. If his income is so low that he is unable to meet his obligations or support his family, if his job is considered low status, or if there is no opportunity for sociable talk on the job, a worker is almost certain to feel alienated. Work alienation is probably the most common reason for referral of *employed* persons to rehabilitation counseling.

Industry is now giving considerable attention to making work interesting and meaningful. But better benefit plans, higher salaries, and improved management policies, administration, and supervision, or even good companionship, are not enough to make a worker feel satisfied (Herzberg, Mausner, and Snyderman, 1959). Although a worker is unhappy without these things, they are not the total answer. Management has learned that giving employees responsibility and recognition, enhancing growth and learning on the job, encouraging a sense of personal achievement, and expanding the possibilities for advancement combat work alienation and lead to job enrichment (Herzberg, 1968). For example, assigning specialized tasks to individuals, enabling them to become experts, promotes responsibility, growth, and advancement.

On the other hand, simplifying jobs by giving each employee just one part of the total operation, as on an assembly line, can break up meaningful slices of work. The assembly line worker tends to regard both his job and himself with contempt (Kornhauser, 1965). Trapped in a monotonous, meaningless, dead-end occupation, he wants to escape that existence or, at least, to see his children escape. The conviction that he is simply an unimportant cog in a giant industrial machine lowers an individual's feeling of personal worth. Ford (1969) gives a graphic example of reversing the process. He enriched the work of fourteen keypunch operators in disbursement accounting (a job with high turnover) by making use of employee differences.

Some were more experienced, brighter and more responsible. Why not give them responsibilities according to their capacities? Before the study, each girl punched approximately one-fourteenth of whatever came in that day. Work came and went. The operator had to meet accuracy and volume standards set by management. But our theory said, "Don't worry about the relation between the worker and her supervisor—primarily. Worry about the thinness of her job—that she is merely a 'hey-girl' for a supervisor who has to get

18

out a payroll." Could we increase the worker's feeling of responsibility and purpose by letting her do the payroll herself? By giving a girl the entire plant payroll to punch, with all the additions, deletions, changes in pay rates, overtime, etc., we created a responsible, gratifying task for her. If the payroll came out completely right, she was completely right, not one-fourteenth right. Each clerk has four, five or six kinds of cards to handle each month. They may help each other and, like secretaries proofreading letters, they verify for each other. Selected clerks set their own verification rates. Some have earned the right to deal directly with other departments instead of going through a supervisor. Only two out of fourteen had earned the right to schedule their own work every day by the end of the ten-month trial, but others showed such good scheduling judgement that they would soon have this responsibility. The experimental group did much, much better than the control group. In fact, after the study only ten girls were needed to run the department instead of fourteen. Turnover and absenteeism dropped appreciably. It is one thing to be ill on a day when your very own payroll is due to go out and quite another to be ill on a day when you are merely one of fourteen girls who get out the same payroll.

This example demonstrates that the early philosophy of the assembly line, increasing efficiency by simplifying the work task, neglected a crucial element: the job satisfaction of the individual worker.

Automation and Leisure

It is widely assumed that significant advances in technology, popularly referred to as automation, are rapidly leading to two major problems: (1) Full employment and full utilization of the labor force will be no longer necessary, and, in fact, we should prepare for full unemployment. (2) There will be no need for unskilled workers or for workers of limited capacity. Russell Nixon (1969) has assembled ample proof that both assumptions are fallacious. Contradicting the first assumption is an analysis (Lecht, 1969) of the manpower required by 1975 to reach objectives in sixteen areas of national concern, as defined by the President's Commission on National Goals in 1960. The general conclusions of this study were:

(1) Full achievement of the sixteen goals by the mid-1970's would require an employed civilian labor force of more than 100 million —some 10 million more than are expected to be in the civilian labor force in 1975. (2) Vigorous pursuit of these objectives in the next decade, therefore, would probably be associated with an insufficiency, rather than a surplus, of manpower. . . . (3) Substantial progress toward achieving the goals considered could be a major factor in creating more and better job opportunities for the country's unutilized and underutilized human resources, especially nonwhites, women, older workers, and the handicapped.

Contrary to the second assumption, the tremendous growth of industrial production has allowed us for the past two decades to deploy a majority of workers in service-producing sectors of the economy, rather than in goods-producing sectors. Moreover, these rapidly expanding service industries are characterized by a low productivity per man hour, as compared with manufacturing industries (Burck, 1970), thus further increasing the demand for manpower. Low-skill jobs, such as nurses' aides, kitchen helpers, chambermaids, and gardener's assistants, abound in these areas, and they obviously provide a fertile field for the development of rehabilitation services. Many persons with psychiatric problems return to high-skill positions. But many, and especially those who are severely and chronically ill, can best find their niche in low-skill jobs. These may not be what one usually considers ego-involved work. But for a person who has not worked for many years, a job, no matter how humble, may be a very gratifying and ego-enhancing experience.

There also is evidence that although "automation reduces skill requirements of the operating work force and occasionally of the entire factory force, . . . automation does not inevitably mean lack of opportunity for the unskilled worker. On the contrary, automated machinery tends to require less operator skill after certain levels of mechanization are achieved" (Bright, 1966). Other studies have confirmed these findings (Nixon, 1969). Although automation results in greater productivity per man hour, many low-skill jobs still remain in factories. Indeed, automation offers many opportunities for manpower utilization.

Carter (1970) feels that the widespread notion of a future increase in leisure and nonwork activities is a myth. He points out two basic factors that tend to increase the amount of work activity. First, trends in management philosophy emphasizing increased job enrichment will make time spent on the job more rewarding than it now is. Second, the low productivity per man hour in the growing service occupations means that more work, rather than less, is becoming available. The result, says Carter, will be that people will choose extended work weeks through overtime or second jobs.

Even if this is true, there is still more to life than work; the search now is on for ego-involved leisure activities. Of course, many persons engaged in ego-involved work do choose to spend a very large number of hours at work rather than leave this time open for leisure. But leisure has become possible for everyone, not just a privileged few; the question is how best to use the time. The rehabilitation worker must often be concerned with helping clients utilize their leisure time in a satisfying way.

Ellul (1968) points out that leisure today "confirms man's general inclination to be passive; we live in a society which turns everything into a spectacle. We experience the most important events as spectators." Obvious examples are television and spectator sports. In addition, we tend to conform in the use of leisure time, even as to where and how we take vacations. Thus Ellul stresses the need for leisure to be completely personal and filled with individual initiative: "Each person must invent for himself his own form of expression. If a man throws his energies into making scale models from a kit prefabricated by big manufacturers, that has no value. On the other hand, a genuine little job of electricity or carpentry can be really formative. We must constantly refuse to take the easy way out, which our society is always offering us. Leisure must be the place where we choose real difficulties for ourselves which we

21

must overcome by ourselves; only at this moment can leisure represent a positive element and contain gratification."

Clinical experience tells us that, while such a point of view has merit, it is unrealistic for many of the people we see. Often they have less difficulty in a structured work situation than in knowing how to play and how to fill leisure time meaningfully. Indeed, making a scale model from a prefabricated kit may be an important step forward for a regressed schizophrenic who has, until now, spent all of his leisure time watching television or staring at the walls.

"Chess, mountain climbing, the violin, the telescope, the easel can and have stretched to the limit the muscles, minds, and emotions of a host of amateurs for as many years and with as great intensity as the demands imposed by most vocations. But to say that play must reach these heights to be respectable is to be ensnared by class prejudice" (Haun, 1967). There is good sense in recognizing that play include such contrasts as television watching and symbolic logic, Bingo and Byzantine mosaics. The price of being an intellectual snob is to be rendered ineffective in helping most people utilize their leisure time.

Some Important Psychological Concepts

The concept of regression is important in the rehabilitation of persons with emotional problems, as in the case of a person who becomes totally dependent upon an institution. This dependence can occur in a total institution, such as a state mental hospital or a prison, or in the community when a person leaves the world of work and becomes dependent on a welfare agency. He retreats to a comfortable, antecedent state in order to minimize anxiety and pain—that is, he retreats from a position of responsibility and independence to one of being taken care of as he was as a child. Regression also is used by people who have had a major traumatic experience—for example, combat in war, death of a loved one, or a major vocational failure—and by people with low self-esteem who are convinced of their own inadequacy, either real or imagined.

22

When the regression is severe and the precipitating traumatic circumstances are mild, we are likely to be dealing with poor ego strength. To put it another way, the more ego strength a person has, the more stress he can withstand before falling back on regression.

In treating regression the therapist or counselor must be alert to the possibility of secondary gain, in which a person finds it socially and psychologically advantageous to remain in the regressed, disabled role, especially if his dependency needs are gratified and he is relieved of his normal work and family responsibilities. Anyone who has lain helpless in a hospital bed because of surgery or a physical illness has experienced difficulty in giving up the dependent role where all his needs were met by the hospital staff, even though there may have been physical pain and emotional discomfort and conflict about being in the dependent role. When the time comes to resume one's normal responsibilities, it can be a wrenching experience, even for the most conscientious and adequate personality.

Resuming one's responsibilities can be especially difficult after an acute psychiatric illness. A patient who is fully qualified in an occupation may be overwhelmed by the prospect of returning to it. To do so may represent either a major step toward independence or a major increase in pressure for which he is not ready. The pressure may be fear of dealing with peers or authority figures in a nonsheltered setting, or fear of increased responsibility or fear of being "too successful" and losing the rewards of illness, referred to as secondary gain. The counselor must be able to recognize when more time and support are needed. For example, a schizophrenic schoolteacher who has had several acute psychotic episodes may need a period of time in a sheltered work placement (see Chapter Five), as a library assistant perhaps, before he attempts to return to teaching.

If the person has limited ego strength and overly strong dependency needs, regression under stress is a likely possibility. If in addition he rationalizes his dependency in such ways as, "I'm entitled to it because I'm a veteran" or "I'm getting welfare because I'm disabled," regression may be hard to reverse. The more rewards

23

he gets from illness and disability, the more difficult the rehabilitation process may be. A pension, increased attention from the family, or being relieved of responsibilities that were difficult to handle in the first place are common examples of secondary gains.

The unusual difficulties experienced by a rehabilitation agency in working with patients from the Veterans' Administration provide an excellent example of secondary gain (Dincin and Swift, 1967).

These patients seemed to have the social symptoms of institutionalism to a degree which even patients in a state hospital do not exhibit. This is partially a result of the good quality of hospital care that veterans receive. There is no physical discomfort associated with their hospitalization. In addition, veterans very often tend to feel that theirs is a special case and that they have a "hero illness." This seems to reduce the motivation for more adequate functioning. The level of pension that veterans with service-connected disabilities receive works as a strong argument against their accepting productive work in the community. It is a matter of simple economics. They can do as well staying home watching television as they can working all day. They are permanently retired and comfortably so. With veterans who have sizable pensions, it is almost impossible to motivate them to work. While we are not advocating a return to "snake pit" conditions nor arguing for a diminution of veterans' benefits, this is a syndrome that is important to note when selecting individuals for extensive (and expensive) vocational rehabilitation services.

The phenomenon of secondary gain is all too familiar to those involved in eligibility determinations of disability, such as for workmen's compensation (Nagi, 1965). A person may be encouraged to emphasize, even to exaggerate, his disabilities in order to receive financial remuneration at the very time he should be encouraged to participate in a rehabilitation program. These considerations have led to the concept of a lump sum payment for disability rather than an ongoing pension. The recipient no longer has a monetary incentive to demonstrate his disability and can now realize his potential for rehabilitation.

Rationalization can offer a way of maintaining self-esteem while at the same time contriving to have dependency needs met. For example, an examination of prison populations reveals that many "criminals" are basically extremely dependent, inadequate people who find in prison an institution which takes care of them, albeit in a way that would not be considered desirable by the ordinary citizen. The prisoner's day is structured; he receives his meals, lodging, and some entertainment; and few demands are made upon him to be independent. Because he is in prison, however, his identity or self-image is not that of a person who wants to be taken care of but that of a tough person whom society cannot handle and therefore has incarcerated against his wishes. His dependency needs are revealed in his anxiety about being released from prison and in the clumsy criminal acts, performed shortly after release, which guarantee his being caught and returned to prison.

In dealing with the regressed and the psychiatrically disabled, we must go slowly and offer something positive to substitute for both primary and secondary gains received from their disability. Transitional facilities, such as sheltered workshops and halfway houses, are essential so that a person need not go directly from total dependency to independence. He is offered the comfort, acceptance, and support of rehabilitation agencies at the time when the institution he depended on is taken away. Even so, the pull back toward dependency and the mental hospital is extremely strong.

A word about guilt is appropriate here. The use of guilt to get others to gratify one's dependency needs is a very frequently used device. Socially and vocationally marginal people are often skilled at evoking guilt in their parents, spouses, and social agencies. This use of guilt is, of course, not limited to people with emotional problems. It is used by almost everyone at one time or another and is graphically illustrated by the stereotype of the "Jewish mother." Whatever one may think of provoking guilt in order to get people to take care of us, it is, at least in some ways, an adaptive, problem solving device. In working with regressed and marginal persons, the results, not surprisingly, are that we feel guilty. Before we can work effectively in rehabilitating chronically disabled persons, we must come to terms with guilt feelings in ourselves. Further, we must be convinced—and not just intellectually—that although pulling a person in the direction of rehabilitation and away from chronic dependency may be painful, in the long run it is beneficial in terms of heightened self-esteem and greater ability to enjoy life. Here, the concept of maintaining high expectations is vital.

A note of warning needs to be sounded for those in the helping professions against what Lipsitt (1968) refers to as overhelp. Our clients make requests, often demands, of us to help them in a variety of ways. Sometimes the client thinks we are omnipotent; sometimes he is merely testing to see how we will react and how realistically we can appraise his situation. "If we are oversympathetic, guilty, and racked by a desire to succor the downtrodden, we may make helping gestures that are inappropriate or detrimental. To promote a person's growth and self-esteem, we must tolerate helplessness in others, even allow a reasonable dependency, but use skill and caution to avoid fostering a deeper, irreversible dependence. Capitulating to totally unrealistic demands, even in the face of appalling misery, only promises that which cannot be delivered."

By overhelping a client, we deprive him of essential opportunities to help himself. He must develop his own sense of achievement and his own ability to handle failure and frustration. A person, in order to be helped, need not be forced to acknowledge his own weakness, be submissive, and accept an obligation. Such conditions seriously undermine his good self-image, and that in turn may foster feelings of anger and resentment toward the "benefactor." Likewise, the helper may find himself despising the "ungrateful" recipient for not responding as he expected; the helper may even feel manipulated and taken advantage of. In responding to an overt or implied plea for help, we must assess whether we are appropriately allowing the person to grow or are overresponding with overhelp because of our own guilt and anxiety.

Carstairs (1969) observes that today everyone expects to be happy; anyone who feels unhappy immediately thinks that something must be wrong either with him or with the state of the world, if not both. We in the helping professions must evaluate carefully the concept of instant happiness, keeping in mind that everyday anxieties and pain can serve as spurs to constructive action. Psychotherapists and rehabilitation counselors must fight the notion that their clients' lives must be free of anxiety and frustration or that all their clients must go directly into ego-involved jobs. Rather, it is their task to see that clients learn how to find ways to handle their problems. Such a process, if meaningful, may often be painful.

CHAPTER 2

Rehabilitation Counseling

Cecile Mackota

✽❂✽❂✽❂✽❂✽❂✽❂✽❂✽❂✽❂✽❂✽❂✽❂✽❂✽❂✽

In the field of rehabilitation counseling, too much energy is expended in debating the merits of specific definitions of the role of counselor. Various camps espouse the causes of the counselor as psychotherapist, as coordinator of the members of a rehabilitation team, as expediter. It seems to us, however, that where rehabilitation counseling is practiced successfully, the counselor is functioning primarily in the area of helping the handicapped solve the issues of occupational choice and vocational satisfaction. He offers a wide range of services and skills geared toward modification of maladaptive work behavior and attitudes which have prevented his client from achieving satisfying work functioning. It is the purpose of this chapter to deal with some of the specific and practical realities of the rehabilitation counseling process.

The vocational field is, in itself, tremendous, demanding a

sophisticated body of knowledge and skills different from those required by the other helping professions. The common goal of helping psychiatric patients to reach more satisfying life adjustment is approached, in rehabilitation counseling, from the avenue of work. Thus the counselor carves out an individual slice of the treatment plan in order to focus on that portion dealing with occupational identification and adjustment. As Freud said, "Work has a greater effect than any other technique of living in the direction of binding the individual more closely to reality; in his work, at least, he is securely attached to a part of reality, the human community."

Rehabilitation counselors, of course, must fully understand the psychodynamics and underlying causes of behavior, particularly the concepts of ego strength and the dependency-independence conflict. But to deal with these dynamics in a "psychotherapeutic" way —that is, to interpret to the client how his behavior stems from developmental factors, to attempt personality reconstruction in depth—is outside the realm of rehabilitation counseling, as we see it. Certainly the counselor needs to take into account what goes on in psychotherapy and how the client's illness, personality problems, and pathological family relationships affect his ability to function and his capacity to work. But the rehabilitation counselor, in his interaction with a client, is committed to the *now* and *from here on* and to working to strengthen the healthy portion of the client's ego. The counselor needs to see the client as he is functioning now in his present environment, what his abilities are, how they relate to that environment, and where modification can help him to get where he is or should be going vocationally.

As a matter of fact, we hold with the idea that the counselor should avoid, as much as possible, reading mental health charts, both at intake and during the course of counseling. The factual material he needs can be obtained from the referral form or letter, which should be brief and contain a sentence or two to describe the presenting problem. Too often the counselor becomes intrigued with a client's pathological history and finds himself involved in it. Dealing with the pathology encourages the client to continue to play the patient role rather than to move into the role of worker. Without

29

getting bogged down in the illness, client and counselor can jointly explore ways to make the maximum use of strengths and abilities. In our experience, the client responds well to the counselor's expectation that the work they do together is to be totally concerned wih vocational choice and adjustment in the future, not with his illness. It is frequently helpful to express this expectation clearly to the client so that "worker responses" are reinforced and "patient responses" are not rewarded. To illustrate with a case: A fifty-four-year-old male client, who had had a long period of service in the Navy, had been unemployed for four years except for some temporary jobs. His wife had gone to work, and he had assumed most of the housework and cooking. It was obvious that he was generally happy in this reversal of the usual roles of husband and wife. However, he was very anxious about the fact he was not working and tense about the image he presented to himself, his wife, and their friends.

He tried to prevent our getting to the realities (his ambivalence about the male role and his comfort in being cared for) by using every interview to intellectualize about his illness, his mother, his childhood, how people had abused him, and so on. I kept pulling him back to the issues with such statements as, "That's all in the past. We're not going to talk about your illness. Let's work on what is going on now and how you really feel and what you want to do." He finally was able to talk about his fears of working and of carrying responsibilities. He also recognized that in many ways he liked being dependent and not working, but he decided to resolve his fears and accept help in finding a low key job, requiring a minimum of responsibility and decision making. With a great deal of support in his transition to the worker role, he has been successfully employed for eleven months. He expresses satisfaction at demonstrating that he is now the man of the family.

Because therapeutic optimism is essential for effective counseling, the counselor must be free to see the client as he presents himself *now*, without being unduly influenced by the detailed psychiatric history contained in the chart. Counselors are hampered by a preconception of the client's work potential; therapists, interested in exploring aspects of illness, frequently present such a "sick" picture that the counselor is discouraged and has difficulty seeing the client's full potential. To cite an illustration: A middle-aged woman was referred to Vocational Services. Over the previous ten years she had been both an inpatient and an outpatient of our clinic services. Her inch-thick record reflected a most chaotic and disturbed family pattern and extensive involvement with various community agencies. She was a second-generation welfare family and her children were being reared on AFDC. At no point in her life had she been independent of welfare assistance. After vocational counseling and testing, she elected to train as a nurses' aide. If the counselor had read her chart before seeing her, I doubt that he would have been optimistic enough to plan with her as he did. Her training record was excellent, and when she graduated, the training institution hired her. She has been steadily employed since then, earning enough to support her family.

From Theory to Practice

Theories and concepts inherent in rehabilitation counseling have had a great deal of attention (Benjamin, 1969; Borow, 1964; Krumboltz, 1966; McGowan and Schmidt, 1962; Malikin and Rusalem, 1969; Patterson, 1960 and 1966; Tyler, 1969). Lacking in the literature is definitive information on how the theories are applied—that is, on how the counselor operates in the day-to-day relationship with clients. We have found that students and new counselors, once they complete their training, are inclined to reject much of what they have learned. They embrace what they call a "down to earth" operating pattern which often results in a haphazard, nonprofessional way of working. Sometimes a feeling of inadequacy in the sense of not feeling equipped to put into practice the principles of rehabilitation counseling is responsible for their rejecting the professional role. In other instances being professional is seen as placing oneself in an ascendant position and "putting down" the client, a line of reasoning which leads to the conviction that one can truly communicate only by being on the client's level

31

and avoiding any distance. Sometimes the use of specific techniques is seen as mechanistic. New counselors feel that what is needed instead to bring about the desired change is solely a personal, helping relationship. If this were the whole picture, life for counselors would be much simpler and there would be no need for the painfully acquired skill and knowledge. Granted that this kind of close encounter between two individuals is therapeutic and an integral part of counseling, there is more to it than that. Specific, practical goals must be accomplished. In working with the client on a goal-oriented task, the counselor's use of various techniques makes possible the focusing on that task and keeps the relationship concerned with what it set out to accomplish. Moreover, with experience, the counselor's self-conscious use of techniques smooths out. They become such a natural part of his operating pattern that his spontaneity and warmth of response are not diminished.

The rehabilitation counselor has no medicine to offer his client to relieve his distress. The only "medicine" is himself, in the dual roles of skilled professional and human being. Fortunately, most counselors learn through experience that the theories developed in the field of rehabilitation counseling are sound and that applying them in a professional way results in effective counseling.

Initially, the new counselor takes it on faith that the concept of establishing a relationship is crucial to effective counseling. Frequently, however, he tries to use this concept without a clear idea of its purpose. Gradually he learns that every transaction between him and his client is important. How he responds—both verbally and nonverbally—can further or set back that relationship. He slowly begins to see that until there is free interaction, until the client, through the interaction, learns to trust the counselor, not much happens. There may be much conversation, much activity, much planning, but usually the real issues are not being dealt with. One of the most common examples of this is the client who is constantly looking for work or going into training programs, but who never finds a job or uses the training. Until he is able to trust the counselor enough to say, perhaps, "I really don't want to work," he and the counselor are wasting their energies.

With many clients the counselor must deal with the deeper significance of work in terms of the independence it represents. When a client assumes a role of dependency, he finds a measure of security and, in many instances, a defense against his fear (real or imaginary) that he is inadequate. Any serious effort toward rehabilitation must deal with this problem. In a free and honest relationship, the client can learn and "sample" other behaviors as well as safely reveal and give up some of his defenses. He can learn new and more satisfactory problem-solving skills, new responses—a new way to experience life.

The counselor must guard against establishing a social relationship with his client. Prolonged social conversation, superficial chatting, and false reassurances do nothing but prevent significant communication. The polite, meaningless, socially acceptable response does not lead easily into a goal-oriented, fruitful discussion. To the troubled person who says, "Nobody would ever want to hire someone like me," a response like "It's not as bad as all that; everything will work out fine" minimizes his problems and sweeps them under the rug. It only convinces him that he will never be understood or get help. How much more effective a response like "You sound as if you really believe that. Can you tell me what are the things you see about yourself that would make an employer feel that way?"

Counselors call on a variety of techniques to bring about a constructive helping relationship. Although certain techniques are useful for all counselors, no one can say definitely what is the right or what is the wrong way to counsel. To be effective, each counselor needs to develop his own style. He must learn what works for him, for he brings to the relationship his own particular personality pattern. He is stilted and uncreative if he attempts to follow precisely and without variation the style used by his supervisor or teacher. He learns to make his own attributes his tools, consciously developing them so that they are available for his use when needed, and he must be given room to experiment, to make mistakes, so that his personal style can develop.

Where one counselor can use humor, for instance, it falls

flat with another. Where one can comfortably arouse and then deal with anger, another needs to approach it very slowly. For example, a troublesome client was being seen by a new counselor, her former counselor having left the agency. Shortly after they were seated, the woman began berating the agency and then began to scream. After many loud, piercing shrieks, the counselor put his hand on her arm to gain her attention and managed to say, "You can't hear me while you scream. When you stop shrieking we can talk." The woman quieted down immediately and that was the beginning of a long and fruitful relationship.

This counselor characteristically responded in a direct and practical way, comfortable with the physical contact. He used this method, which was effective for him, to set limits and help the client to regain control of herself. Limits could have been set in other ways. The same approach might have been disastrous for a counselor with a different personality style.

As style differs from counselor to counselor, so must the same counselor vary approaches with different clients. One client might benefit from a long-term introspective relationship; another, geared to action and unused to introspection, can benefit more from dealing with concrete factual material and very early job finding.

The most basic and, at the same time, the most sophisticated of techniques is the use of verbal responses to clarify, focus, or encourage the unfolding of relevant material from the client. The counselor learns to function on two levels: on the surface, he is fully involved in the interchange; on a deeper level, he evaluates the meaning behind what is being expressed so that his responses are not haphazard or inadequate. He observes verbal and nonverbal expressions that reveal his client's coping methods and the way he relates to other people. By sharing his impressions, he helps his client to become aware of unsuccessful patterns of behavior and to explore new ones. By his own verbal and nonverbal communication, he gives messages about what material to pursue, drop, or clarify. He keeps to the purpose of their relationship, which is to solve occupational adjustment problems.

In this connection, Miller (1966) provides a pertinent framework for conceptualizing verbal responses. He distinguishes five types of "verbal regulators" useful to counselors:

(1) Remarks that encourage continued speech ("green light" responses): "I see. Tell me more." (2) Remarks that keep the focus on a topic already presented: "What did you think of that?" "What other sorts of things have you done with your hands in the past?" (3) Remarks that clarify communication and ensure that the counselor and client understand each other: "You seem to be saying your boss wouldn't rehire you because of your bad back." "Are you saying that this particular job made you anxious and uncomfortable?" (4) Remarks that channel the discussion or bring the client back to an important issue previously glossed over: "Perhaps we can discuss this later. Let's go back to what you mentioned a minute ago about your co-workers." (5) Remarks that present information: "You are at the thirty-fourth percentile on the Otis."

I would add a sixth: Remarks that reward "worker" responses. Supportive statements such as, "It must have been difficult to take on that added task, but you did it. Great! That's progress" encourage appropriate behavior. Conversely, not picking up on "patient" responses should discourage patient behavior.

In the same way, nonverbal responses encourage or inhibit material. Facial expressions, gestures, or a marked show of attention or inattention are all in the counselor's arsenal of nonverbal responses. Looking away, as a means of ignoring fantasy material, is often a most effective way of discouraging it.

Fully as important as verbal response is the ability to remain silent, to give the client time to move at his own pace and think through what he wants to say. Too often counselors jump in to "explain" what the client is saying, breaking into his thought process and, frequently, stopping a flow of important material. Out of his own anxiety, the inexperienced counselor thus conveys the message that listening to what the client has to say is not enough. The frustration this can engender in the client may well prevent the relationship from developing. To be really listened to is often a unique experience for many of our clients and one that enhances feelings of self-worth.

On the other hand, blindly adhering to the principle that periods of silence must be interrupted *only* by the client can put too much burden on him. He may be confused and need help to focus; he may be immersed in fantasy; he may be thinking about something of importance but reluctant or embarrassed to say it. A lengthy period of silence may create too much anxiety and immobilize him. A simple question, such as "What are you thinking about now?" can often free him to talk again.

We have found it useful for counselors to employ a high expectation attitude. When care is taken that expectations are at a realistic level for each client so that failure is not inevitable, our experience shows that clients respond, upward or downward, to the level of expectation the counselor indicates. If the counselor confidently expects the client to behave like a worker, not a patient, worker behavior is almost always presented. Conversely, if the client gets the message that little is expected of him, he is likely to function at a low level. The client exhibits little upward striving to achieve in the absence of the conviction that he is able to achieve.

Many of the clients in our workshop still spend part of each day in a day treatment center. We are daily impressed with the contrast in the behavior we observe, depending upon whether they are in the workshop or in the center. In the workshop, patient behavior is not tolerated, and in the expected role of worker, the client behaves as a worker. The same client, in the role of patient in the hospital or day treatment center in the morning acts like a patient, exhibiting symptoms we never see in the workshop the same afternoon. He responds to the expectations of the setting in which he finds himself.

The counselor must not overlook the client's emotional strengths and weaknesses in helping him plan for a vocation. The client's intellectual capabilities and aptitudes may be far beyond what he is emotionally capable of doing. In setting expectations, the counselor may more appropriately be helping his client lower work goals to a level where he can function comfortably. For instance, a thirty-five-year-old graduate engineer had three psychotic episodes, each, in our estimation, related to the demands of the job. He became involved in vocational rehabilitation counseling at the time of his third hospitalization. He was able to decide to accept a job at the post office and has worked steadily and has been free from illness for more than four years.

Another technique at the counselor's disposal is confrontation. In the security of a trusting relationship, the client can accept and use information that makes him aware of how he comes across to other people. Further, in confronting him with discrepancies between action and verbal statements, the counselor can help him recognize self-defeating behavior: "It seems to me that you are saying you want to get a job more than anything else, but you are doing everything possible to prevent your being hired. Let's look at what happened in that last interview." The counselor must be very sensitive to when the client can tolerate this honest and open approach and to when the relationship is sound enough to make it possible. In our experience, confrontation has the added merit of being a limit-setting device. It clearly spells out to the client that you are not going to allow him to "con" you. Thus, he does not have to continue, with you, a method of coping that he has used in a damaging way. For some clients, this kind of limit-setting can open up possibilities for less self-destructive behavior.

The judicious use of directiveness is another effective tool. Counselors bend over backwards to avoid being labeled directive, a term which has become synonymous with bad counseling. Yet there are many instances when the counselor can "lend" his own ego strength for the time the client needs it. In dealing with issues of overt behavior, particularly with regressed clients (although not necessarily limited to them), giving special directions and advice can be the technique that gets through and effects change. The directive approach has the merit of honesty and concern which sometimes rings truer to the client than a subtler approach. A very depressed, disorganized client can respond better to "Go comb your hair and clean up your face before you go back on the workshop floor," or to "Change your clothes and clean up before you go out on that interview," than to "How do you feel about grooming?"

For example, a twenty-eight-year-old workshop client was so self-deprecating that she was unable to tolerate the mildest praise. She was an excellent worker, learned quickly, and was clearly ready to move out into employment. She had good clerical skills and thus had a marketable occupation. She was, however, convinced that no employer would consider her and countered every effort to move her by saying, "I'm not ready. I'm slow and inefficient and don't believe I'm as good as you say." It was apparent she could not, on her own, take any step toward employment. The counselor approached the client on a morning she was appropriately dressed and told her that whether or not she believed she could be a good employee was to be disregarded in this instance. She was to use and trust the counselor's opinion of her and to act on that. She was directed to go out on an interview that morning. With much trepidation she complied, was hired by a local firm, and has been on the job over a year. Without this direct approach she might still be in the workshop, deprecating herself.

Counselors frequently express fear that they may be harming a client by being directive. Years of experience have convinced me that if there is true concern and respect, which cannot help but get across to the client, the likelihood of doing harm is remote. I believe that the rare counselor who cannot get involved enough to experience this liking and concern should leave the field.

Sometimes the counselor must take a calculated risk. Bringing to the surface hidden anger or hostility directed at the counselor is often the only way to achieve a breakthrough. My own experience with a young woman, with whom I was getting nowhere, illustrates this point. I had been seeing a twenty-four-year-old client for a period of about eight months. Although many of her problems had been worked through and she had maintained a job for four months (her first steady job), she was still having difficulty with her employer. We were having very little success in pinpointing the problem. She maintained a facade of sweetness and good nature in which

I sensed buried anger, and I purposely made remarks aimed at making her show anger toward me: "You're making that sound awfully simple." "You're not telling me the whole story." After a number of such remarks, she spitefully said she was not going to stay, got beet red in the face, and stalked out, slamming the door so hard the building shook. She arrived at the appointed time the following week, and from then on our relationship was on an entirely different footing. She was able to talk about her anger directed at me and her employer as authority figures, and she admitted that she occasionally "blew up" at her employer, using vile language. We could now work together at her handling anger in small doses. She is still working on the same job.

In order to trust his counselor completely, a client must be sure that nothing is hidden from him and that he is not being manipulated behind his back. This means that the counselor must be open about whatever concerns the client, the good and the bad. This means the client should be involved in conferences about him, or, if that is not appropriate, he should at least be aware of their being held, of who is present, and of their purpose. This means he should be present at meetings with his parents or other relatives. Indeed, the counselor should not have such meetings if the client does not approve. This means the client should know the results of tests and evaluations, good and bad. Too often the counselor withholds information for fear it may harm the client. To learn to be open himself, the client needs the counselor's demonstration of openness.

Vocational Testing

At the point in the counseling process when the client is able to look at himself objectively in terms of his own vocational assets and liabilities, the counselor should make tests available. It is at this time that they become purposeful and are an effective means of helping the client to focus on specific occupations, to eliminate others, and to plan more realistically. The counselor gains objective information that allows him to help the client in making an appropriate choice. In general, tests furnish clues which may reinforce choices or open up new areas of vocational exploration. In many instances, they also serve to give the client a feeling of security about the choice he has made.

In his use of tests, the counselor needs to be fully aware himself and be certain that his client understands that tests are only another tool to assist in his client's self-appraisal. There are, unfortunately, no push-button methods that give complete answers to vocational problems. Tests serve only to add information to what has already been perceived. Although tests may reveal potential, other factors, such as the client's emotional problems, may make it clear that some aptitudes cannot realistically be utilized.

Interpretation of tests is a highly sensitive area and the counselor must guard against drawing conclusions for the client in presenting test results. The object of the tests is to give the client information he can use in reaching his own decisions (Patterson, 1964). For example, a client whose goal was to be a teacher had a personal-social score on the Employee Aptitude Survey at the thirtieth percentile. Telling her that eighty per cent of teachers scoring at the thirtieth percentile do not succeed is far different from saying, "You should never attempt teaching with a score like yours." By involving himself in testing, the client is, in a sense, putting himself on the line. Natural anxiety before and during the tests, and strong emotional reactions to the results, must be expected and dealt with. In the case referred to above, a long cherished ambition to be a teacher had made "I am a person who will some day be a teacher" part of the client's self-image. Needless to say, seeing the test results was a devastating experience for her. Before further planning could be done, a number of sessions were needed to help her accept the reality of her capabilities.

Counselor Roles

One of the most important roles a counselor must play is his role as a model. The counselor, in relating to his client, shows him a way of behaving which he may use as a pattern for his own behavior. The counselor demonstrates how one person can relate to another in a positive way even though their values and needs are different. A vital aspect of this is the counselor's not feeling compelled to maintain a formal, stiff, "professional" posture which can only serve as a barrier between himself and his client. The counselor must feel free, within the context of a professional relationship, to respond as he would naturally; he need not suppress all affect, nor should he equate professionalism with being constricted and non-spontaneous. Through his behavior, the counselor says, in effect, "This is how you relate to another human being. You will get more if you risk more and show yourself as who you really are. You can be accepted even if you reveal yourself." Further, the counselor demonstrates by his own behavior that work can be fulfilling, as well as enjoyable, and that a person working at what is right for him can have a good life. Moreover, it is evident to the client that there are times when the counselor is frustrated and angered by things that happen during his working day. The way in which the counselor handles these frustrations is an object lesson for the client and prepares him for the reality that even in satisfying work one must accept some negatives.

A major role which most definitely distinguishes rehabilitation counselors from workers in the other helping professions is that of being a resource person. The counselor must have a wide knowledge of the occupations, including an intimate knowledge of how and under what circumstances they are practiced. Counselors must be aware of groupings of jobs so that skills which are transferable can be utilized in vocational planning. Further, the counselor develops an in-depth working knowledge of the particular personality traits that are required or contraindicated for specific jobs, so that he can help his client make an appropriate choice. The counselor must bring together the individual needs of the client and all the reasonable possibilities open to him. Unless the counselor is knowledgeable in the field of occupations, his service is limited and he does not live up to the expectations the client has in coming to him for help.

In order to acquire this knowledge, counselors need a curiosity and interest in how products are made and how things get done. In his daily living he is alert to these aspects and stores away many bits and pieces of information about occupations that he can use in his work. He also pursues this in his interviews, since his clients are really his best source of information; they can describe, in the detail he needs, work they have done. Such information gathering serves a dual purpose; the counselor learns a great deal about his client from the way he talks about his work; and he enhances the client's self-image by encouraging him to expand on an area he knows more about than the counselor. Gradually the counselor accumulates information about countless occupations in the best possible way—from those who have done the work.

In addition, each counselor should start to build a personal occupational library as early as possible. Much information is available, free of charge, from industry and various governmental agencies. The *Occupational Guide,* for instance, published and revised frequently by the Research and Statistics section of the California State Human Resources Commission, is invaluable; it covers all aspects of hundreds of occupations and gives sources of further information. Similar publications are available in other states. A vast supply of rich material is available to any counselor who sends for it.

In his role as resource person, the counselor must be familiar with nearby schools and training institutions and be able to evaluate their usefulness to particular clients. Further, he needs to be aware of funding sources of all kinds so that training is available to those who cannot finance it themselves.

Beyond this, a counselor must keep up with the state of the labor market in his locale so that clients are not preparing for unmarketable or outmoded occupations. He must assess clients' past work experiences to find those which are particularly marketable now. The search can be as exciting as a detective story, depending upon the attitude and creativity of the counselor.

When clients are ready for employment, the counselor becomes a teacher. He helps clients to learn the most effective way of seeking a job. He shows them how to fill out applications, how to enhance their chances of passing entry tests, how to prepare a résumé, if one is necessary, and how to behave in employment interviews to maximize their chances of success with emphasis on alternate behaviors in differing circumstances. The best way for clients to learn these things is to do them. Role playing is exceedingly helpful in providing a dress rehearsal for real job interviews. Following this, the counselor can help the client use every job interview as a learning experience: "When you were asked this question, your response was _____. Might you have said this or this or this?"

Clients are particularly sensitive to questions about mental illness by employment interviewers. What is important is that the counselor help the client sort out his feelings and decide how he wants to respond to such questions. For most of our clients, telling a lie is not the best method, even if it results in being hired. They experience so much anxiety about being "found out" that they rarely achieve comfort and satisfaction on the job. We prefer to help the client accept the reality that certain employers do not hire ex-mental patients. He must seek out the increasing number who do. We then work on how he can handle himself to impress such employers with his being on top of his problems. Most effective, we find, is a simple statement, without elaboration, such as "Yes, I have had emotional problems for which I have been treated. I am now fully ready to work." Frequently, anxious elaboration of details concerns the interviewer more than a history of mental illness, per se.

In placement activities, we believe that for most clients the counselor can be most effective by not intervening with the employer. A client thereby acquires job seeking skills that are useful to him, and his self-esteem is vastly increased when he finds his own job. Moreover, a counselor who intervenes for him gives him another mixed message: he is judged ready to become an independent, productive citizen, and yet he is taken by the hand and responsibility assumed for him again.

In our experience, clients who are really ready for work—and the independence it represents—have little difficulty finding a job, depending, of course, on the state of the labor market. Clients who do not succeed point up that our efforts have been lacking. We have accepted an appearance of readiness; we have, perhaps, been too eager to move or we have not been sufficiently perceptive to read the messages behind verbal expressions.

Sometimes the counselor may not be understanding enough of crises and the emotional implications involved. He may not recognize that the client lacks the emotional strength to handle both his life situation and vocational planning. The client may need time to resolve his life problems before he can involve himself in work, no matter how ready he may appear on the surface. Recently, one of our new counselors was working with a young mother whose husband had deserted her during her pregnancy. She was a keypunch operator and had a good employment record prior to the birth of her child. She seemed bright and alert, and asked only for help in organizing a job search. She expressed eagerness to work and a strong desire to get off welfare. The counselor and client engaged in an active program of preparation for interviews, and the client followed through on all leads but was not hired. The counselor was baffled by the client's inability to find a job. Not until he had had many meetings with her did he realize that her self-image had been shattered by her husband's rejection. She felt completely worthless, and she presented herself so poorly to employers that they would not hire her. Other factors also needed to be dealt with, as for instance her being alone, with her dependency needs now no longer being met.

Another client had moved from the state hospital to a halfway house in the community as his transitional residence. At the same time, he was referred to our workshop. Three months later, the client had made considerable improvement at the workshop so that his counselor arranged a work assignment for him in a local industrial plant. Shortly thereafter, the client became overtly psychotic and was rehospitalized. What the counselor had not taken into account in making his arrangements was that, at the same time, plans were being made at the halfway house to move the client to independent living. The client was thus faced with the necessity of making two major adjustments simultaneously. This example again highlights the importance of considering the events in the client's personal life when planning vocational changes.

Sometimes counselors are unwilling to recognize that some people do not want to be rehabilitated. They expend a great deal of energy on rehabilitation and produce nothing but frustration. Conversely, sometimes the counselor is prone to give up too soon on some people, particularly the very chronic. A client who had been in a state hospital for more than twenty-five years had been in our sheltered workshop for over a year. His progress had been minimal. His counselor, thinking that the client had gone as far as he could go, was prepared to close the case as a failure. A different counselor recognized the man's potential and accepted very small gains over a long period of time as significant. After another year in the workshop, followed by a sheltered work placement in industry lasting several months, the client entered competitive employment where he has now done well for nine months.

Although we are committed to the concept that the treatment of choice is helping the client to find his own job, we recognize that, for some clients, this is unrealistic. The counselor must take a more active role in the placement of the very chronic person, who cannot tolerate the competitiveness and anxiety involved in job seeking, by talking with supervisors, educators, and employers. Of course the counselor must be very sure that his decision to intervene for the client and do direct placement is based on the client's need and not on the counselor's own anxiety for success. He must guard against cutting short the client's opportunity for personal growth and development that come from learning how to find his own job.

Doing direct placement requires the counselor to develop still another set of skills; he must have not only knowledge of the labor market and industry in his area but also the ability to use selling techniques with employers comfortably. The counselor often shies away from such "unprofessional" activities, but he must be able to function in this role to serve severely handicapped clients effectively. The rehabilitation counselor must feel secure enough in his professional identity to see his role as encompassing such activities in addition to counseling in his office. For those clients not ready for competitive employment, the counselor must be willing to try new methods of helping them toward as much vocational functioning as they are capable of achieving. Sheltered placement programs in industry, discussed in Chapter Five, are one way to accomplish this.

Another important role of the counselor is that of collaborator with other rehabilitation facilities. He needs to communicate clearly the purpose of the referral to the other agency and the specific areas in which his client needs help. Workshop directors will gladly attest to the needless waste of time and effort caused by improper or incomplete referrals. For example, when a client is referred to a workshop with the counselor's stated goal "Client needs daily activity." Small wonder that both client and workshop staff flounder! Contrast this with "Client has had a poor employment history. Always loses jobs because of difficulty with authority. Needs to work on accepting and using supervision." Here, from the very beginning, all concerned know what their task is and where they should focus their efforts.

For maximum use of a rehabilitation facility, it is essential to identify what problem areas need to be worked through in that setting. The client needs a clear concept of how his placement can be of help to him. When he is unsure, and merely says, "My counselor sent me," the activity is frequently nothing more than a babysitting arrangement. When he knows that he is in a workshop because "I never could get along with my co-workers," or "I lost every job I've had because I fought with the boss," or "I've never been able to stand being in a shop with other people for eight hours," the first step toward modification of his behavior is accomplished.

We cannot overemphasize the importance of continued involvement, once the client is placed in a workshop or other sheltered activity. Not much growth can be expected from the person who is dumped into a workshop or training program and does not see his counselor for months on end. The kind of support a counselor gives by seeing his client regularly, discussing progress (or lack of it), and planning for the future can do much to determine the outcome of the placement. Sustained interest of the counselor, alone, is a powerful motivating factor.

The counselor also has the role of collaborator when he works with other professionals involved with his client. If he is part of a mental health treatment team, he can bring the hard facts of work into the clinic atmosphere to prevent the underwriting of unrealistic vocational goals. He can present facts to assist in therapy and obtain in turn useful information that will make his work more effective. Vocational goals should be in keeping with treatment goals for a patient so that counselor and therapist work within an integrated plan.

The counselor's role does not end when the client is placed in employment; at the very least, contact should be maintained for several months until he is stabilized on his job. The counselor should understand his role as more than simply compiling statistics of clients placed in employment and thus "rehabilitated." The client needs to have someone with whom to discuss and resolve problems that inevitably arise during the initial period of adjustment on a job. He must be encouraged to bring to the counseling session problems that might otherwise cause him to be fired or to give up and quit his job. The initial period of adjustment on a job is critical. For the client, failure at this point, after he has involved himself in the rehabilitation process, is devastating; he may only now have allowed himself to believe that success on a job and independence might be possible for him.

Even when the client is stabilized in employment, the counseling process may have only just begun. That real growth can continue in the context of an ongoing counseling relationship is illustrated by the case of a twenty-nine-year-old single girl who had never been able to hold a job. She was referred to psychiatric vocational services with a diagnosis of "inadequate personality with possibly some mental retardation." It was felt that she could not make good use of community resources such as the State Human Resources Division without specialized help. At that time she was living with and being supported by a brother, an engineer. Her mother had deserted the family in her infancy and her father, a successful architect, had remarried and left the home. She seemed to be an embarrassment to her father and brother, and the father, although he lived in the area, rarely saw her and had given her no help since she failed in her first year of college.

After evaluation and testing, this client was placed in our workshop for four months. She was then moved to a kitchen helper training program. Our object was to help her lower her goals to a point where she could find some success in working. We felt that she had been pushed beyond her capacity by her family. The kitchen helper training program led to a minimally paid temporary job. Later, she took a night job helping to care for an invalid for room and board and a small salary. She was able to move out of her brother's home and become independent of him financially. These were giant steps for her, and she handled them well.

This client has now been supporting herself for three years, managing on a marginal income. She has, throughout this period, been seen by her rehabilitation counselor, at first weekly and later monthly. She changed jobs and worked successfully for two years as a maid at a hospital. She expressed dissatisfaction with "always cleaning up other people's dirt" and became increasingly depressed when she could see no way out of this situation. She was anxious to learn to do some work that would make her feel better about herself. She is presently enrolled in a nurses' aide training program. The goals of counseling with this woman are to bring her along slowly so that she may realize her potential. At the same time, recognizing that the family culture stresses achievement, it has been the counselor's role consistently to reinforce the notion that it is acceptable, and desirable, to work at a low level occupation. By preventing her from overreaching herself, it is possible to help her gain the sense of satisfaction and achievement through work for which she longs.

This case demonstrates that in dealing with chronic patients, particularly, the counselor must be flexible enough to remain actively involved for long periods of time in order to achieve lasting results. Premature case closures often undo the gains made. Sometimes the client's first experiences with employment are only steps toward final successful vocational adjustment.

When one considers the rigorous demands of being a rehabilitation counselor, it becomes apparent that a person must have strong convictions—and a strong back—to enter the field. The frustrations are plentiful, but so are the rewards. The *Occupational Guide* (California Department of Human Resources Development, 1970) spells it out, though in somewhat idealized form, in describing a Rehabilitation Counselor: "In addition to specialized knowledge required for this occupation, he must have sound judgment, the ability to make decisions, imagination, initiative, sensitivity in human relations, and resourcefulness. Moreover, he must possess persistence in the face of setbacks, ability to create an atmosphere of hopefulness in the presence of human distress, and the capacity for personal growth and development."

CHAPTER 3

The Rehabilitation Workshop

Isadore Salkind

$\ast\mathcal{S}\ast\mathcal{S}\ast\mathcal{S}\ast\mathcal{S}\ast\mathcal{S}\ast\mathcal{S}\ast\mathcal{S}\ast\mathcal{S}\ast\mathcal{S}\ast\mathcal{S}\ast\mathcal{S}\ast$

It is my intent to help rehabilitation workers in the field of mental health make effective use of rehabilitation workshops. The following two chapters describe workshops as a rehabilitation resource. This chapter identifies what actually happens in a workshop—how people are referred, what they do there, and how plans are carried out for placement—and examines the goals, basic assumptions, and problems of the rehabilitation process itself. Chapter Four explores the ways in which economic factors affect the life of the workshop and offers some proposals for the future of the workshop. Throughout the discussion, our aim is to help the rehabilitation worker develop guidelines as to what to expect from the workshop, what are the limitations of a workshop, what is the function of workshop personnel, what information the workshop needs from the counselor in order to get the most benefit for his clients.

Generally, clients referred to a rehabilitation workshop are deemed not ready for competitive employment, on-the-job training, or a work experience placement in private business or a government agency. They are, however, ready to take a first step toward a vocational goal. Such clients present a myriad of problems that prevent them from working or make them fail on a job. The sheltered setting of the workshop enables rehabilitation personnel to evaluate and deal with problems such as inappropriate behavior on the job, inability or unwillingness to follow orders and deal with authority, poor grooming and personal hygiene, faulty work habits which lead to low productivity and ruined work products, irregular attendance or tardiness, and inability to socialize with co-workers. How is this accomplished? I will begin by briefly taking the reader through each phase of the operation of a modern workshop, from intake through post-workshop placement.

The first step in bringing the client into the workshop is the intake process, where physical, psychological, social, and vocational problems are evaluated. The intake process is crucial and will have a weighty impact on all that subsequently happens. Using the medical, psychological, and social data he has on the client, the intake interviewer, usually a professional worker, evaluates the client even before the client is seen on the work floor. His written evaluation enters the case record and can strongly affect the way in which the client is worked with in the workshop.

Many workshops do not have an intake counselor or interviewer and must rely solely upon the information sent by the referring agency. This is regrettable for numerous reasons. A good intake worker helps the client understand what the workshop has to offer and makes his entrance into the workshop a positive experience. In particular, it is at this time that the client can best be helped to identify the problems he is going to be working on. The client's motivation can be immeasurably enhanced by the assurance of the intake worker that the workshop will try to help him solve these problems. The client's expectations of the workshop are pretty well set at intake and profoundly affect how he will use it. Without an intake worker, initial case records are often inadequate and seem to set a precedent for case records that later are lacking in details about the client's progress in rehabilitation, making measurement of movement forward or backward difficult and unreliable. As standards continue to rise, however, more workshops are hiring rehabilitation counselors who perform the intake function as part of their duties.

Once the client enters the workshop, he may be placed either directly in a work station or in a prevocational unit. If he is ready for a work station, he then does real work for which he is paid. If initially he needs to be placed in a prevocational unit, he does a variety of simulated work tasks—known as work samples—selected from existing work tasks or jobs to determine on what level he is functioning and what his skills and attitudes are. Workshops vary in how long they have a person doing work samples, from only a portion of a day to as long as a couple of weeks. Work samples are generally intended to identify hand-dexterity, physical capacity, ability to understand and follow instructions, eye-hand coordination, and particular individual occupational skills. The variety of work tasks available in a contract workshop at any given time is limited and does not provide the range of work demands necessary to fully test the client's potential in all fields.

There is a growing interest in work sampling to assist in occupational choice. Workshops are being used to evaluate hard core welfare clients and the culturally disadvantaged, whether or not any physical or psychiatric handicap exists. Work samples, unlike standard pen and pencil tests, do not place a premium on verbal skills. Thus, evaluations using work sampling can be more valid in assessing the vocational potential of persons whose true potential is not revealed by standard tests. These persons can become involved in and make good use of work sampling because it is concrete, lacks abstraction and does not depend on verbal ability. What the client can do, not what he can say, becomes the criterion.

The Rehabilitation Workshop

When work samples are carefully set up to simulate actual jobs that exist in the current labor market, they can be helpful in determining what are realistic possibilities for the client. Even the best work samples, however, cannot duplicate the dynamics of real work, where the interaction between supervisor and worker is critical and wages, the social factors of work, working conditions, and co-worker relations are real and compelling. Work samples, when combined with a paid work experience, can be helpful, but they should not be used as a substitute for a work experience. Doing real work resulting in a useable product has an authenticity that in itself is a powerful motivating force. Further, work sampling like other techniques which attempt vocational evaluation is profoundly affected by the extent to which the client anticipates the possibility of a real job following the evaluation. If the client feels there is strong likelihood of a job, he becomes involved in the evaluation experience, and his involvement is reflected in his performance.

If he is initially placed in a work station rather than in a prevocational unit, the client works on tasks in the same manner as other workshop clients. However, he is closely observed for the same factors of work capacity and skills, as he would be in work sampling. When the client first enters the workshop itself, having come from or bypassed the prevocational unit, he is likely to be moved from one job to another over a period of several weeks, as part of a diagnostic evaluation. His capacity to accept a work situation, his general attitudes toward the structure of work, and his ability to accept supervision and to relate with co-workers are observed. The workshop staff in this early period makes initial judgments about whether it can work effectively with this particular client, about what kind of problem he has in work, whether it will take a short time or a long time, and whether there are other services that the client needs either before or during the work experience. Sometimes the worker has physical problems that interfere with work—for example, the prescription for his glasses must be changed. If such matters are not corrected, the workshop staff does not get an accurate picture of the client's potential.

If the workshop staff feels that it can effectively work with the client beyond the diagnostic period, he is assigned to a work station, and his actual work experience begins.

Under what circumstances would the workshop staff decide that the client should not continue beyond the diagnostic period? Ordinarily, the client makes it clear through his behavior whether or not he wishes to go beyond the diagnostic period. If, for example, a client manages to arrive at the workshop only three or four times in a two-week period, the workshop can safely conclude that he is not yet willing to accept a workshop experience. It is unwise to plan continuation until the client's ambivalence is resolved. It is, of course, quite possible that the client sees himself as wanting to work but does not see the workshop as the right place for him. The workshop staff must then return the client to the referral source for further counseling and decision making.

Sometimes the decision to go beyond the diagnostic period, or not to, is related to other concerns. Workshop directors or intake workers frequently receive requests like the following from counselors: "Say, John, I have a young nineteen-year-old fellow whom I'd like to send to the workshop for a diagnostic period of three weeks. I'd like to find out what he is like as a worker. If he looks pretty good and seems stable and regular, that's all I need to know, because I have other plans for him which involve training. I don't want to risk the expense without first learning more about his work habits."

In such circumstances many workshop directors would probably go along. Some questions that should be raised about such a referral are: Will the client be psychologically prepared to invest himself in what he sees as a temporary activity? Is the client being given a real opportunity to decide what should happen to him? Will the workshop be able to give satisfactory answers about the client's work performance and ability in so short a time? These questions cannot be answered in the abstract. The workshop director or intake worker should carefully evaluate such a referral and not blindly agree to it. The workshop is in a dilemma in such situations; refusal to accept the client may alienate the counselor and result in a decrease in the number of referrals from the agency. This could mean substantial economic loss for the workshop.

The workshop simulates a realistic work environment as closely as possible in order to prepare clients for work situations elsewhere. The workshop is essentially a small business, bidding competitively for contracts and meeting delivery dates and quality standards. It generates production demands, receives pressures from sub-contractors, which are transmitted to supervisors and in turn to clients. The workshop tries to offer a wide variety of work experiences, ranging from simple assembly and packaging to complex production sequences. Services such as food handling, messenger work, janitorial and maintenance work, wood and metal work, machine operation, and office and clerical experience are offered. In some workshops, nonhandicapped workers are employed at full salaries and work side by side with clients. They serve as role models, help create a realistic work environment, and give the shop a consistent core of productive manpower to meet contract deadlines. Work programs have been developed outside of the workshop, also, in such areas as maintenance of motels and bowling alleys, gardening, and reforestation. This trend relates the work experience to possible placement in competitive employment and offers an alternative to the feast or famine economics of the traditional subcontract described in the next chapter.

Throughout the work tryout, the workshop staff identifies strengths and weaknesses and helps improve the client's work performance. Regular evaluations measure the client's progress. The appendix describes the application of work adjustment techniques in improving the client's behavior and attitudes. An understanding of the role of the workshop foreman can help professionals dealing with workshops to understand the specific intent of work adjustment techniques. Two other works are recommended to the interested reader. *The Requirements of Effective Sheltered Workshop Supervision* (Barton and Barton, 1965) is an excellent study in the field of workshop supervision. *The Rehabilitation Workshop Foreman and His Role* (Barton, 1971) is one of the best tools available in the workshop training area.

While the client is in the workshop, he comes in contact with the workshop foreman more often than with any other member of the staff. The foreman has more influence than anyone else on the client within the workshop setting; he is an authority figure, serves as a role model, and has the responsibility for evaluating the client. A workshop foreman can have tremendous influence on the work behavior of a client, but we cannot say what particular training discipline produces the type of foreman desired. It is idle to argue whether only a psychologically trained person or only an industrially trained person should work as a foreman in a rehabilitation workshop. The essential concern is whether or not he is the kind of person who can create the strategies and interventions on the work floor which force changed behavior on the part of the client. Neither training in industrial skills nor the usual psychological training guarantees success (see Appendix). Furthermore, the foreman must be seen by the client as an authority figure, a boss with the power to discipline and reward, a boss such as the client could expect to find elsewhere. Although the foreman in a modern industrial setting is not the autocrat he might have been a few decades ago, he still is an authority figure.

The rehabilitation client must recognize the difference between a foreman and a counselor so that he can anticipate to some degree how he will be treated in the world of work outside the workshop. The two roles have sometimes become blurred, with the foreman taking on the role of counselor to such an extent that he is compromised in his ability to correct client behavior. By the same token, a counselor who unwittingly accepts the responsibility of disciplining a client becomes an authority figure in whom the client may feel less free to confide.

Following is a typical example of what happens all too frequently in workshops: A workshop foreman came into the office of a vocational counselor complaining, "Look, I've warned that client three times about leaving her work station to go over to talk to the girls in the other end of the shop, and it hasn't stopped. I can't seem to find a way to control it, and I think maybe you should handle this."

At this point the counselor might say, "Send her in to me to talk about it"; or she might say, "Send her home for the rest of the day. Also, tell her that if she wants to talk about it with me when she gets back I'll be glad to see her." Either approach will almost certainly lead to a situation in which the client sees the discipline as coming from the counselor. The foreman lacks confidence in his ability to handle a problem in a rehabilitation workshop setting or, perhaps, has difficulty being an authority figure. Although the foreman goes back to the client with the decision, the decision has in fact been made by the counselor and the client knows it.

In this situation, just as in a usual supervisor-worker situation in industry, the foreman ought to simply go ahead and make the decision. The foreman should not have to confer first with the counselor before disciplining a client—the decision is the foreman's to make and should be seen as such by foreman, counselor and client. The foreman should have sufficient understanding of the rehabilitation process generally and the client's problem in particular to impose whatever discipline is required. He need not immediately inform the counselor of his action unless he believes it has precipitated a crisis for the client. Regular conferences between workshop staff and counselors provide the necessary feedback to the counselor. The foreman need not become overinvolved in dealing with the client's reaction to the discipline. It is the counselor's job to handle the client's feelings about all aspects of work, including his workshop experience.

Frequently the foreman has not been helped to feel adequate to handle his job. The foreman has less formal education than the counselor and is not trusted by the workshop administration and the counselor to make intelligent decisions about clients. The workshop administration is responsible for training the foreman and helping him feel more secure in taking the initiative to applying work adjustment techniques to change clients' work behavior.

During the work experience, counseling is usually offered so that the client understands and is able to benefit from what he is experiencing in the workshop. The counselor, whether employed by the workshop or by another agency, helps the client to accept the realities of the work situation, not as an apologist for the management but as a helping person who is interested in seeing the client succeed as a worker. Although a client's response to work is complex and not easily compartmentalized, the counselor limits the content of counseling to work-related issues. The counselor is the person responsible for seeing that the rehabilitation goals are carried out for each client.

The counselor and workshop staff collaborate to help the client change his self-image and discard negative attitudes resulting from past failures. The counselor does not try to help the client make basic changes in personality or character structure but to help the client become a better worker. If the client needs psychiatric treatment in order to become an effective worker, the workshop counselor finds the psychiatric resources which are needed. He does so not necessarily because he lacks competence but because working in this area is inappropriate to his role as a rehabilitation counselor.

Most workshop programs do not emphasize or offer training in specific occupational skills. Rather, they concentrate on adjusting attitudes toward work and improving work habits. Workshops have been told forcefully and frequently by employers in industry that industry will be happy to offer the skill training required if the workshop can produce a dependable person who is willing to work and do what he is told. The great majority of people who fail in work do so for reasons other than lack of specific occupational skills. But emphasis on adjustment rather than skills, although essentially correct, leaves serious placement gaps for workshop clients.

The jobs for which employers are willing to offer training are generally unskilled or semiskilled jobs which, although they may pay fairly well, do not offer possibilities for advancement. Also, because of educational deficits, many workshop clients cannot qualify for entrance into the trade and technical schools which train for the skilled jobs available. Consequently workshop clients generally do not get placed in good jobs. In order to meet this problem, the government has created a number of training service grants which have encouraged workshops to set up training programs in occupations like custodial work, food service, clerical and office machine operation. These programs, although limited in number, have proven successful in preparing clients for some of the skilled jobs available. They are also unique in that the client's income is not based upon his productivity but rather is funded directly by the grant. It is a training income rather than a wage, and so it is substantially higher than most workshop wages.

When the client has derived maximum benefit from the workshop and is ready for competitive employment, plans must be made for his entry into a regular job. Placement of clients into jobs has always occurred in workshops, but workshops have just begun to consider it a serious part of their programs, especially for clients with serious and chronic psychiatric problems. In the past, workshops did not formally accept placement as a responsibility because other agencies, such as state departments of rehabilitation and state departments of employment, were and are still charged with that obligation. Many workshops still do not do a great deal of job placement.

But placement is important to the workshop in a number of respects. For one thing, the placement function is a major source of feedback in telling the workshop staff whether or not its work with the client readies him for competitive employment. Suppose the workshop tells a department of rehabilitation counselor that a particular client is ready for a job. The counselor places the client who then fails, and the workshop learns the hard way that its evaluation techniques were not effective. The more sophisticated workshop directors would rather have feedback from their own placement workers than from external sources. Another reason why placement is receiving more attention is the underlying knowledge that agencies which purchase services from workshops are more likely to use workshops which offer direct placement services. This is not hard to understand, with counselor caseloads heavy and so much emphasis given to numbers of people placed. It is hard to understand why so many workshops in the past failed to provide such an important, needed service. The more astute directors who realized that having their own placement workers guarantee a flow of clients for whom fees are paid have garnered the lion's share of community interest and governmental support for their workshops.

The workshop director must be committed to the goal of improving client work performance, not to the goal of operating a successful business. Modern business techniques and equipment are essential, but only as a means of implementing the major goal of rehabilitation. If the director's energy is directed toward making the workshop a successful business, rehabilitation suffers. Compounding the problem is lack of training and sophistication of the staff. Most workshop staffs do not have field training and must be helped to develop on the job. Unless there are adequate financial resources, many aspects of the program are not adequately staffed. For instance, without a high ratio of supervisors to clients, it is impossible to pay close attention to client performance and behavior. If the foreman on the work floor is responsible for more than ten or twelve clients (in some cases even ten may be too many), he is not able to work intensively with them.

The workshop director must be able to create a psychological climate which encourages good work behavior without being punitive or grim. This climate is created not by written rules but through the values which are transmitted by the behavior of the staff and the director as they go about their own tasks.

The referring agency also plays a part in determining the effectiveness of the workshop. Does the referring agency provide pertinent medical and psychosocial information? Does it specify concerns it has about client work performance? Is it willing to be involved in client evaluation? All these issues have a sizable impact upon effectiveness in dealing with clients in the workshop. If counselors at the referring agency lack expertise, the workshop cannot deal as effectively with the client as it might otherwise.

The more specific the questions raised by referring agencies about client behavior, the more likely it is that such questions can be answered directly by the workshop. In many instances, referrals to the workshop are vague and ill-defined. Frequently, counselors use the workshop as a dumping ground for difficult clients for whom they have not been able to accomplish a satisfactory placement in competitive business. Such referrals could be appropriate if those referring understood and accepted the need in such cases for a long-term sheltered placement in the workshop. But referring counselors often maintain unrealistic expectations. Consequently, the workshop staff feels frustrated and taken advantage of. Ultimately, such referrals lead to deterioration of the relationship between the workshop and the referring agency.

I have briefly mentioned some of the problems that interfere with making a workshop effective. Even if the problems were resolved, what about implementing the rehabilitation process itself? Does the workshop staff know what goals it is striving for? What does it really want to accomplish? Each workshop staff may come up with different answers, depending on the assumptions it makes about what can make the rehabilitation process work. Here are my ideas, the assumptions I feel are important if a workshop is to be effective. They apply to all workshop clients, not just to those who will become transitional and competitive in a relatively short time.

The first assumption basic to a workshop setting is that you leave basic personality structure alone and focus instead on changing work behavior, attitudes, and expectations. Techniques used in a workshop, while effective, are designed not to remake the worker but to effect enough behavioral changes to help him hold a job or, at least, to improve his function in work. Without this assumption clearly in mind the workshop staff can easily become confused about its goals, and this confusion can disrupt operating techniques. We must recognize that the workshop is not the only rehabilitation tool available and that it is not an all-purpose tool. If the workshop staff understands where its true effectiveness lies—in changing maladaptive work behavior—the workshop is more successful in its overall goals.

For example, a workshop client has a great deal of underlying hostility masked by a facade of passivity and compliance. Although he is full of rage, this man has his anger well under control and is only dimly aware of it. He has held many jobs, but only for short periods; each job has been characterized by his enduring without complaint what he has seen as unreasonable demands placed upon him by supervisors and co-workers. Inevitably there has followed a sudden, violent, angry outburst which has led to his quitting or being fired. The workshop in conjunction with his counselor can help this client look at each situation more objectively and voice in an acceptable way his complaints about those demands which are in fact unreasonable rather than allowing his resentment to build up to an explosive level. The facade of passivity can be left alone. The goal is not to help the client understand the genesis of his hostility, nor is it to help him "express his anger" and free himself of his pent up rage. The goal is to help him modify his behavior sufficiently so that he can hold a job. If the client desires to change his basic personality structure, he should turn to psychotherapy, not to the workshop.

The second assumption is that workshop clients can perform at a higher level than the one at which they currently function. The workshop staff must believe in this approach and find ways of transmitting its expectations so that all people within the shop are geared to attempting to do a better job. With good supervision, this approach need not create undue anxiety and can be used to express confidence in the capacity of the client to improve his performance.

A third fundamental assumption is that within certain limits practically all clients can respond to mature treatment and achieve self-improvement in many areas. If the workshop staff does not set up this assumption, it is babysitting rather than seriously trying to effect improvement in work behavior. The following case history illustrates the dynamics of what happens when expectations for client performance are not high.

H.B. is a severely impaired cerebral palsied person in his late twenties who lives in a city distant from his parents with no visible support except Aid to the Totally Disabled. He has been a workshop client for many years. H.B. has always been a difficult person to work with, unkempt, defensive, frustrated because he is bright but unable to make effective use of his intelligence. His workshop productivity, because of his impairment and negative attitudes, was ten per cent of an industrial worker's. After several years of very trying experiences and many behavioral crises, he was given to a supervisor who believed H.B. could be helped to improve. She helped him set goals in production and in self-cleanliness and tried to help him recognize that, though impaired, he could improve and, of equal importance, derive gratification from work.

H.B. doubled his production and made faltering, uncertain steps toward improving his appearance. He slid back many times but was able to respond to others' belief in him as long as supervisory understanding was built into the relationship. In this situation, gains in productivity also helped to raise his self-esteem and thus contributed to improving his functioning in areas other than work.

The fourth assumption is that, if it is to bring about improvement, rehabilitation must involve more than the mere exposure of a client to a work situation. Clients frequently do achieve some improvement in their work performance simply through exposure to a work situation. The work situation is dynamic; it causes clients to relate to many other people and creates a social climate which gives approval for good performance. However, although the work situation itself may act as a catalyst for the client, he needs more than that. There must be feedback and confrontation concerning the nature of his performance in order to achieve maximum improvement. Frequent interaction between client and foreman is needed, with techniques designed to bring about the desired work improvement. For each client in the workshop there should be a plan which has been carefully thought out and which is utilized to strengthen behavior. Such a plan, although it must not be rigid, must include tactics and strategies worked out by the counselor, foreman, and other professionals concerned with the welfare of the client.

There are specific interventions which are sometimes characterized as "manipulating the work environment," a phrase which is often misinterpreted. What is sought is the active effort of the supervisor or foreman to create situations and make changes in the work environment so that the client is forced to respond to the changed situation in a way that is different from his previous way of responding. Some standard ways of doing this are changing the group in which the client operates, isolating him, and putting pressures upon him through the production system so that he has to relate his work to that of other people. Most of these situational techniques are dependent, however, upon the foreman's knowledge of the client's weaknesses or limitations in work.

An important aspect of the situational technique is the emphasis it places upon nonverbal communication. Words are readily misunderstood by people; under stressful situations, we tend to hear only what we wish to hear. The workshop foreman, therefore, utilizes his eyes, his body, gestures, and other nonverbal techniques to transmit his attitudes and feelings about the client's performance. For example, let us assume that a foreman is working with a client who continually comes back late from coffee breaks and who has ignored the usual admonition. The foreman may decide, the next time this happens, to sit at the work station and do the client's job. When the client finally shows up, the foreman, instead of rising, simply continues to work. The client stands by, uncomfortable because the other workers see the foreman doing his work. When the foreman thinks he has made his point, he may get up and walk away without saying a word. He has managed, nonverbally, to get across a clear message. Further he has mobilized the social pressure of other clients to convey disapproval of the undesired behavior.

Other examples may help explain the process of manipulating the work environment. Let us take the case of Peggy, a young woman in her late twenties who was referred to the workshop by the Association for the Retarded. She became part of the in-crowd and quickly came to enjoy the social aspects of the workshop; in fact, her social life could not be contained within the ordinary coffee and lunch breaks. In addition to talking on the job, she found it necessary to take frequent trips to the bathroom (one or two trips per hour), for which there was no medical reason. These trips cut down her productivity. Although she wanted to earn more money than she was making, she did not see her frequent trips to the bathroom and the socializing along the way as being related to her loss of productivity, even when it was explained to her. After a number of efforts failed to curtail the excesses, the foreman set up a simple chart with two columns and horizontal lines, one line for each working hour. The first column was headed "trips to the bathroom"; the second column was headed "units of production." The client was asked to tally each trip to the bathroom in the first column, and in the second column her production was entered. She was encouraged to wait longer between trips. This was done matter-of-factly, leaving the responsibility up to her. In a month's time, it became evident to her that there was a definite relationship between her trips to the bathroom and her production. Despite some fluctuations, there was steady improvement—that is, a decline in trips to the bathroom and increased earnings due to higher production.

Another example: when others whom she knew at the workshop became employed outside the shop, it was difficult for Ann to understand why she, too, could not get a job. In addition to some personal characteristics that would hinder her, her production seldom got above sixty per cent and averaged around thirty-five per cent. One effort to relate her production to the reality of that demanded in competitive employment was handled in the following manner: The job on which she was working involved rolling six-foot lengths of gift wrap paper on a cardboard core, then wrapping a plastic sheet around the roll and heat sealing it in place. The finished roll was placed in a shipping carton of twenty-four. Production was kept track of in this manner. To help her understand what a competitive worker would have to complete in an hour, the number of shipping cartons required to hold the established units-per-hour was placed to her left, rather than having the leadman make up the cartons as they were needed. At the end of an hour, she could see what still had to be done. Over a period of time, this method helped her to increase her production, without loss of quality, but she was never able to complete the entire number. With counseling and other similar efforts, she was able to see the limitations of her performance as a competitive worker at that point in time.

The following experience illustrates the role of the workshop staff in determining whether or not the client is ready for employment: Bob was a friendly, nice looking young man, twenty-one years old, who had a short work history of several briefly held jobs. After about four weeks in the program not much change had occurred in his poor attendance and lack of punctuality. At this point, he was assigned to a new foreman, a woman, with whom a warm, positive relationship developed. During the next six weeks, he corrected most of his inappropriate behavior and had been working independently and well as a dishwasher and busboy in the workshop cafeteria. Support, encouragement, challenge, and praise from his foreman always seemed to bring renewed growth and progress. It was finally decided at one evaluation that the counselor responsible for placement should work with him at job finding. He soon became employed as a dishwasher. Within four days, he was out in the street again.

Fortunately, some sharp questions were asked about what testing had been done to determine this man's readiness for employment. A harassed, dollar-conscious boss who let his employees have it when he was angry had triggered Bob's undiscovered temper. Words and a punch at the boss terminated his employment abruptly. The happy relationship at the shop had showed what Bob could do under comfortable circumstances. Before exposing him to another possible failure, other pressures and demands should have been made to tease out undesirable behaviors so they could be dealt with constructively in the workshop.

While all clients should be considered possible candidates for competitive employment, some individuals cannot reach this goal. The fifth assumption, then, is that preparation of such clients for long-term or permanent sheltered employment is one important contribution of the transitional workshop. Problems arise when the workshop staff sees all clients as being on the road to competitive employment. For example, John, a slight, quiet man of thirty-seven, has been in the workshop for five months. He had spent the previous nine years in and out of state hospitals and had been diagnosed as a chronic, undifferentiated schizophrenic. Although his behavior in the hospital had been reported improved as a result of drug therapy, his release was associated more with the need to empty the hospital than with any specific hope that John had achieved a stable remission of symptoms. John comes to the workshop regularly and on time, and he does what he is told. He exercises no initiative but works willingly at whatever he is assigned. He understands instructions and follows them, but after five months in a work adjustment program he is still afraid to use his own judgment and is bewildered if the work is changed slightly or if new demands are made. Clearly, the staff must recognize that competitive employment is not a realistic goal for this man, at least for the foreseeable future. Otherwise, both the staff and the client will experience repeated frustration, and both will feel that they have failed. A positive outcome would be placement in a long-term sheltered work situation with both staff and client experiencing a sense of accomplishment. In this sheltered placement, the same concern should be shown for John's further development as a worker, with the continued application of work adjustment techniques. A judgment of limited potential should not mean that the client receives no further services.

The sixth assumption which the workshop must make is that material rewards are important to the workshop client. There are ways of testing client work performance which do not pay the client. Such tests can describe many aspects of work behavior, but they cannot duplicate the dynamics that are created when people are paid for their work and when their work improvement is reflected in improved earnings. This, of course, is not to say that material rewards are the only way of motivating workshop clients. It does say that money rewards are a very significant aspect of workshop motivation and that there are almost no clients, no matter how low their level of functioning in the workshop, who cannot respond to improved pay as a result of improved work. A good workshop makes a conscientious effort to pay clients in relation to performance at a rate comparable to that of nonhandicapped workers doing similar work. This is more difficult to achieve than one would suppose. There is a great temptation in some workshops to pay clients less because the workshop is permitted, under the law, to pay less than the minimum wage. Then, too, some workshops do not sufficiently measure and record the amount of work each client does and, consequently, do not have a real basis for comparing his work performance with that of the nonhandicapped worker. Additionally, low bidding on the subcontract price will result in unfair wages to the client.

That the client should participate fully and effectively in his own rehabilitation process is the seventh crucial assumption. This means that he can be trusted to participate as an equal in all of the sessions which are held to evaluate his particular work effectiveness. By and large, there should be very few situations from which the client is excluded. One exception might be a meeting to resolve staff disagreement about the client's performance or potential or how to work with him. Thus, the client is not burdened with conflicting staff messages.

If the client is made aware of his difficulties on the work floor, it then should come as no surprise to him to hear them openly discussed in an evaluation session. A note of caution: the more the session is free of psychiatric jargon, the more meaningful it is to the client. His inclusion in evaluation and planning sessions emphasizes his active involvement in the rehabilitation process. If real change is to be expected, the client cannot simply be a passive recipient of services.

There are, of course, other points at which the client's active participation is basic to the rehabilitation process. Many people are referred to workshops not because they wanted to come but because someone else felt that it was important for them to come. For example, a client referred by a counselor from the state department of vocational rehablitation may think that going to a workshop is a waste of time. He may feel, quite reasonably, that he cannot afford to refuse because he may be denied other services as a result. Many clients who accept vocational training programs in which they are not interested because they feel that they must go along with the counselor either abandon the training program or complete it half-heartedly. They do not seek a job in the area in which they were trained because they were not interested in it in the first place. For reasons such as these, it behooves the workshop staff to find ways of probing the extent of client interest in order to determine, when the client first comes to the workshop, whether he is coming because he wants to improve as a worker or because he is going through the motions to please his parents or the counselor.

That there must be a constant flow of work—preferably with variety and scope—is the eighth assumption made by workshops. To translate this assumption into practice, however, is another matter. Probably the major problem facing workshops today is lack of an adequate supply of work. This thorny problem, elaborated upon in the next chapter, is one of the most critical factors in the life of the workshop. Few workshops have been able to cope with this problem; most of them continue to have serious intermittent disruptions. Either a system of governmental and industrial set-aside programs which guarantee the flow of work must be developed or funds must be provided to rehabilitation agencies to purchase existing businesses which manufacture and sell a finished product or provide such services as gardening, janitorial and institutional food service.

Any rehabilitation process must have a basic philosophy, a set of principles that guide its operation. I have set forth 8 basic assumptions for the rehabilitation workshop: (1) The major focus is on changing work behavior, attitudes and expectations while leaving basic personality structure alone; (2) there must be a belief that workshop clients can perform at a higher level than the one at which they currently function; (3) that practically all clients can respond to mature treatment and achieve self improvement in many areas; (4) that simple exposure to a work situation is not enough, that there must be a sufficient quantity of intelligently planned supervision consciously directed at modifying work behavior; (5) that preparation of persons, incapable of competitive employment, for long term or permanent sheltered employment is one important contribution of the transitional workshop; (6) that material rewards, usually money, are a significant aspect of workshop motivation and replication of the real world of work; (7) that the client should participate fully and effectively in his own rehabilitation process; (8) that there must be a constant flow of work, preferably work with variety and scope. It is my contention that these assumptions, diligently applied and put into practice, can make the workshop a meaningful first step, and often the crucial step, in the rehabilitation process.

CHAPTER 4

Economic Problems
of Workshops

Isadore Salkind

Although workshops have been in existence for more than a century, their complexion has changed as a result of increased demands being placed upon them. Today the emphasis is on evaluation, work adjustment, and transition to either competitive employment or work placements. The workshop movement did not begin with these concepts, nor was it so complicated as it is now.

Workshops developed out of charitable motives. The first workshop in this country began in Boston in 1840 at the Perkins School for the Blind. In the beginning workshops were concerned mainly with giving blind and physically handicapped people work activity. This is not surprising as it has always been easier for us, as a society, to nurture those whose handicaps we can see and to take care of them rather than help them toward independence.

A major push occurred after World War I when many injured veterans returned with handicaps which did not permit them to take competitive jobs. As the industrial society grew, the number of on-the-job accidents resulting in serious handicaps encouraged the development of rehabilitation centers. These centers developed programs of occupational therapy designed to help injured persons rebuild muscles and develop dexterity needed for physical recovery. But even as these occupational therapy programs were being developed, it became apparent that injured people who had once worked were not interested in ceramics, leather work, or simple crafts. Activities that were samples of real work, and, finally, actual workshops, became part of the rehabilitation centers. As a consequence, there are now more than one hundred rehabilitation centers in the country which have workshops.

Although the workshop movement is still concerned with physical disability, emphasis has shifted from physical to psychological factors. It came to be recognized that physical damage leaves psychological scars. Also, as society became more complex, there was an increasing realization that emotional factors were extremely important in work. Research led to the further recognition that most people who fail in work fail not because they lack work skills but, essentially, because they are unable to get along with other human beings in the work situation. While this is unquestionably an oversimplification of the problem, it is important to note the shift in emphasis which took place in the workshop movement. This shift furthered the development of work adjustment techniques based on the notion that changing attitudes toward work and attempting to modify behavior in the work setting was much more important than teaching occupational skills. The Jewish Vocational Service of Chicago, in the early 1950's, pioneered in this field and achieved major gains in working with unemployable people whose previous history had been marked by emotional disturbance as the primary cause of unemployability.

With the Vocational Rehabilitation Act of 1954, workshop

development received considerable support and encouragement from the government. Large numbers of workshops were started, and it was during this period that they began to become a growth industry. This growth in numbers of workshops, however, is somewhat deceptive. Most of the growth which took place in the 1950's was in the establishment of small workshops. The total workshop population has not grown as much as might have been expected from the increase in the number of shops. Although workshops serve as many as two hundred thousand people during the year, there are fewer than one hundred thousand people in workshops throughout the country at any one time (Button, 1970). Goodwill Industries, which numbers about 140 of the 1,200 existing workshops, serves more than one-third of these people. Approximately half of the workshops in the country have fewer than fifty people in them. (Because we do not yet have a full taxonomic picture of the workshop movement, the figures cited here are approximate.)

Another aspect of the growth that has occurred since 1954 is the establishment of a large number of workshops for the retarded. There are probably more than three hundred such workshops throughout the country. Workshops for the retarded tend to be small and parent-dominated in terms of influence exerted by the executive boards. They tend, also, to be minimally concerned with developing real vocational skills among the retarded workers. These shops are generally established as part of an agency, such as a school, whose concerns for the retarded are in several dimensions, so that their chief emphasis rarely is on the vocational development of the retarded worker.

In addition to Goodwill Industries workshops and workshops for the retarded there are approximately seventy-five workshops for the blind, more than one hundred workshops which are part of rehabilitation centers, and seventy-five to one hundred workshops within mental hospitals, including Veterans' Administration hospitals, throughout the country. An increasing number of workshops located in the community follow the model pioneered by Jewish Vocational Services in Chicago, which specializes in short-term adjustment techniques (Gellman et al., 1957). These workshops have had a great impact upon clients who fail in work because of psychological problems, ignorance of what is demanded in the world of work, problems in interpersonal relationships, and so on. In large urban communities, there is a trend toward bringing into workshops such new populations as the disadvantaged, the exoffender, the drug addict, and the dropout from society who has decided that he wants to return to the world of work.

Additionally, the Salvation Army and the Volunteers of America number approximately 150 workshops which, like Goodwill Industries, salvage and repair clothing and household goods as the prime work activity. The sale of these goods is the chief method of raising funds for operation. Also developing throughout the country is a significant number of community workshops, sponsored by groups of agencies, which work with a wide variety of handicapped populations.

Also on the increase is a large number of workshops which are called work activity centers. They are frequently attached to workshops for the purpose of accommodating severely disabled people who do not work the full day. In them, nonwork activities such as recreation, social therapy, and occupational therapy accompany the work experience. The main emphasis, however, is upon paid work for a substantial part of the day. Although wage regulations prescribed by the Wages and Hours Division of the Department of Labor are different from those prescribed for workshops, work activity centers may be counted as workshops.

Rehabilitation Versus Business

Because the workshop is a business as well as a rehabilitation facility, economic factors assume great importance in most aspects of workshop philosophy and practice. In practice, it is not possible to identify a single conceptual framework for workshops because of the number of different types of workshops operating with different sets of assumptions and goals. There is, however, a common denominator: Paid work is the main activity in the workshop.

There are exceptions to this general rule. They are the workshops run by county or other government departments in which the worker is receiving a welfare stipend and does not receive direct payment from the workshop. He usually receives only a few small extras, such as lunch money and carfare, beyond welfare support. In such cases, the workshop has difficulty in developing motivation, since the person cannot gain monetarily from working in the workshop. Despite this handicap, such shops have succeeded in moving many workers into employment. Those who administer such workshops admit, however, that their efforts are hampered because the client does not receive an immediate, tangible reward for working.

Psychologically, the meaning of paid work in the workshop rests in the duplication of normal social dynamics which marks it as being different from therapy in the customary sense. The workshop attempts a double responsibility: It uses paid work as the tool for rehabilitation and modifying work behavior; at the same time, in attempting to duplicate the reality of a business setting, it finds itself actually running a business—paying wages, accepting contracts from industry, and dealing with problems of quality control, procuring subcontracts, competitive pricing and bidding, and controlling inventory. While the two concerns are not always in conflict, developing a balanced approach is difficult, to say the least. In the absence of adequate financial resources, rehabilitation concerns of the workshop often are diminished. The costs of business and of rehabilitation must be separated, for the rehabilitation costs cannot be passed along to the firm that lets the subcontract to the workshop.

Sometimes financial concerns conflict with concern for the rehabilitation of the client—for example, if several workshop clients are ready for placement at a time when there is pressure to meet a contract deadline which the workshop staff feels cannot be met without them. Obviously, the variables in a workshop are tremendously complex as compared to those in a private business. First, the client load is a less predictable workforce than is found in a private business. Then, too, the board of directors of a workshop often is concerned with the entire community. Because its goal is not monolithically directed toward making a profit, the board may not define its objectives clearly, creating conflict between the board and the executive director in many instances. On the other hand, because the board is obligated to raise funds, it is often more conscious of money matters than is the executive director and less informed about rehabilitation programs.

The community is also involved in the life of the workshop. When the community is called upon for financial support, it becomes concerned about the value of the workshop program.

Additional uncertainties are created by the work flow into most workshops. Workshops suffer either feast or famine. The majority of workshops do not have a stable flow of work at contract prices that enable the workshop to offset overhead and ordinary business expenses. Many jobs taken by the workshops are short term and introduce hidden costs—for example, the costs of frequent changes of jigs (devices for holding work materials in a fixed place in order to facilitate production) and fixtures. Although these changes add variety to clients' work, they build in inefficiency because clients are not able over a period of time to increase their proficiency as they would on long-term contracts.

Many short-term jobs are speculative business promotions in which the margin of profit permitted to the workshop is small. Many jobs are based upon simple hand labor operations which companies have not been able to mechanize in their own plants and for which they seek to pay as little as possible. Workshops accept these jobs because they have such difficulty in getting enough work that they fear to refuse the marginally priced work, even though in many instances workshops could ask for and obtain more money from the companies. The image of the workshop as a source of cheap labor is difficult to change and its consequences are an uneconomic work flow, one that could not be tolerated in the average business, small or large.

In the workshop, as in large organizations, the individual who runs it influences the shape of the organization. The workshop director must understand rehabilitation, administration, and business. He is a generalist rather than a specialist. His main function, no matter how small the workshop staff, is to put together a team which understands the complex job which the workshop should perform. There is a shortage of personnel trained for the job of worshop director, and consequently there are many directors who so lack understanding of business administration as well as rehabilitation that the development of the workshop movement has been hindered. Many workshop directors do not have the experience to deal with the economics of the subcontract and at the same time manage the workshop in such a way that economics do not defeat rehabilitation goals.

What has been said of directors is, to a certain degree, also true of workshop staffs. There is no prior vocational training for foremen in rehabilitation workshops. Many foremen have come from other occupations in which interpersonal skills have not been as important as they are in a rehabilitation workshop. This lack of training has created serious problems for workshops and has been only partially remedied; there are still few facilities for training workshop staff.

From the point of view of managing a business, the nature of the rehabilitation program involves many unusual considerations. What types of contracts are suited to the rehabilitation needs of the client? Should the clients be permitted to do all phases of the work, even if it is more costly to do so, or should complex operations be turned over to minimally handicapped people? Should more machines be introduced? Can the rehabilitation clients be permitted to ruin subcontract materials that belong to the subcontractor? How should the loss be made up by the workshop? Can the workshop provide a broad enough rehabilitation program? For example, training in areas which are valuable to the client is not always available through subcontract, and the income from such training is usually less than the cost. These are problems that must be resolved if a workshop is to provide a sound rehabilitation program.

Complicating the life of a workshop even further is the fact that no one variable operates by itself. The workshop director cannot operate independently of the board, his staff, the referring agencies, the rehabilitation needs of the clients, the business aspects of his shop, and the needs and wishes of the community. These factors are interdependent upon each other to such a degree that their management becomes, at best, a compromise. Ideally, the client should be the center of concern and all other factors should be secondary. In reality, he is only one of the variables in the workshop equation; his rehabilitation must share priority with the financial needs of the workshop, the administrative needs of the workshop director and staff, and the work flow. Often the fiscal needs, rather than the client, assume a central position.

Conley, in *The Economics of Vocational Rehabilitation* (1965), had this to say about the sheltered workshop:

Probably the low wages paid in most types of sheltered employment discourage any increase in the number of sheltered jobs. Undoubtedly, low earnings are due in part to the lack of ability and skill of the disabled, but they may also be due to inefficient or inexperienced management, which is reflected in an inability to obtain profitable subcontracts, an inability to organize production, a poor choice of products, and poor pricing policies. Other factors that may be causing low earnings are lack of capital, which necessitates using old fashioned machinery and expensive hand methods, and the small size of the average workshop, which makes it difficult to handle sizable jobs or to guarantee delivery dates. Moreover, few of these establishments have the resources or the industrial contacts that are necessary if all possible sources of work are to be tapped. The solutions to the problems of sheltered employment are not yet in sight. Possibly state rehabilitation agencies should organize more homework and workshop projects. Possibly a central agency should be set up to act as a focal point for obtaining large subcontracts and apportion such work to the appropriate workshops. These agencies might also distribute finished products for marketing. Perhaps the best solution would be to encourage the development of sheltered employment in industry.

While Conley's comments are not inaccurate, they are, in my opinion, unduly pessimistic. Unfortunately, they probably do reflect a widespread view of rehabilitation workshops. Although they are primitive and beset with problems, workshops are a dynamic tool in rehabilitation. A more balanced view of the possibilities of workshops in rehabilitation can be obtained from a study of workshops in other countries. A book which provides an account of workshops abroad is *Principles of Industrial Therapy for the Mentally Ill* (Black, 1970). Black's firsthand description of European workshops indicates that work therapy is an important part of the social welfare system.

To the workshop, from the point of view of profit and loss, each client represents a certain degree of deficit. If the client is only half productive, the workshop needs twice as much staff, space, overhead, and material handling to produce as much as would be expected from nonhandicapped workers. The double cost is not completely offset by wage-and-hour exemptions which permit the workshop to pay less than the legal minimum wage. And, unlike most small businesses, the workshop usually begins with extremely limited amounts of money, outmoded equipment, and almost no money available as risk capital. Because the workshop cannot predict the level of work skills of its clients, it is able to offer little more than unskilled hand labor, which imposes serious limits on its ability to realize income from business. Also, when the subcontract is bid, it can only be obtained by bidding competitively against nonhandicapped labor. Most companies using workshops do not pay them more than the competitive rate, and many try to pay less.

Rehabilitation services impose costs which cannot be met from business income alone and, consequently, demand an additional source of support. Workshops need rehabilitation counselors and evaluation personnel. Frequently, they also utilize either full- or part-time services of psychologists, social workers, and other professionals in support services. Rehabilitation income, in the form of fees, does not usually cover such costs.

It is important to recognize not only the economic impact but the overall influence which state divisions of vocational rehabilitation have had on the development of workshops. Workshops have been almost a creation of state departments of vocational rehabilitation (DVR). Because DVR counselors need services—work evaluation, work adjustment, work experience, and occupational training—for moving people into competitive employment, they have encouraged workshops to develop. Consequently, many workshops are oriented toward transitional work experience—that is, toward screening clients and preparing them for competitive employment. DVR's need to move people quickly into competitive employment has made its mark on the development of the workshop. DVR's reluctance or inability to pay fees for people who cannot readily become competitively employable has left a gap in support services for clients who are more seriously disabled and who cannot soon, or perhaps ever, become competitively employable.

There are many factors in the relationship of workshops with DVR. First, the degree to which a workshop is used is dependent completely upon the wishes of the individual counselor. Even if his supervisor indicates a desire to use the workshop, the decision is dependent upon the individual counselor for its implementation. The workshop must therefore work with many different counselors in order to develop continued predictable demand for its services.

The decisions which govern counselor choices in use of workshops have very clear implications for the economic picture of the workshop and frequently influence the nature of the rehabilitation program as well. Counselor satisfaction or dissatisfaction is a crucial element and is at the heart of some of the most serious problems faced by workshops. If the counselor does not understand the nature and purpose of the workshop, he may underutilize it or not utilize it at all. Counselor concerns with the workshop are varied. Counselors want a realistic evaluation of work performance, including client exposure to a variety of work at varying levels of complexity. Counselors often want the workshop to play a role in the placement of the client or sometimes to provide long-term employment for the client if he is not capable of achieving competitive employment.

In most states, the amount of spending by DVR for case services is not maintained at a year-round level. Frequently, two or three months before the end of the fiscal year, DVR runs out of money and those counselors who were sending clients to workshops must suddenly discontinue such purchase of services and hope that the workshop is able, somehow, to continue working with the clients without a fee. In most instances, the workshop cannot do so. The fee which is paid by DVR rarely covers the full costs of rehabilitation services. Some states have begun to experiment with other methods of paying for workshop services through bloc funding arrangements—that is, purchase of services through contracts on an annual basis. Such planning is a significant advance over other methods of funding since it enables the workshop to plan its program and budgeting annually.

Another problem is unsophisticated accounting in the workshop; little use is made of cost accounting techniques which are capable of separating the rehabilitation costs from the business costs. A workshop which is well run and operates with good business techniques and a level of technology which compares favorably with industry may cost less to operate and appear to have a lower rehabilitation cost than a workshop with inefficient business practices. The inefficient shop may be including, in its rehabilitation costs, some costs which are actually the results of poor business management. If, as in some states, DVR pays rehabilitation costs that are residual after business costs have been identified, it punishes those workshops which do better than the less efficient workshops in business.

The problem of procuring work severely limits the usefulness of the workshop as a rehabilitation tool. We have spoken of the feast or famine which most subcontract workshops experience. It cannot be overemphasized that even though many workshops have made advances in this area there has been no overall solution to the problem. In some states, workshops have been able to form procurement associations for the purpose of obtaining more work for the shops. For the most part, however, the results have been disappointing. In many instances, workshops share the misery of poor subcontracts with the client and are unable to choose work based on its training value to the client or even to realize a reasonable monetary gain.

A number of problems are peculiar to particular workshops. For example, workshops like Goodwill Industries, where the sale of salvaged goods is the main source of support of the operation, emphasize sheltered employment rather than transition to competitive employment. As a result, large numbers of handicapped workers who could be placed in competitive employment become dependent upon the existing structure. The need for salable salvaged goods creates urgent pressures to keep the best workers at wages below what they could earn elsewhere. Some salvage workshops have begun to develop rehabilitation-oriented approaches, with added rehabilitation staff and emphasis on transitional employment. However, the old emphasis is still the predominant one for most of the salvage workshops. One positive and perhaps ironic note: Many of the salvage operations, because they have had to support their activities from business income, have developed personnel more attuned to the realities of retailing, merchandising, and production than has the ordinary subcontract shop, dependent upon nonbusiness income for much of its support.

Workshops for the retarded have a different set of problems. They did not start with the idea of becoming vocational training centers but originated out of parental concern to provide constructive activities for their retarded offspring. From this beginning, not without difficulty, they developed a vocational direction. It became apparent that work solutions for the retarded were possible. A major obstacle to their implementation has been the reluctance of many parents to see their retarded children trained and placed in low status jobs, even though these jobs may be the limit of their capabilities and even though such jobs would give them a sense of independence and self-worth. Many middle-class parents prefer the fiction that their children are students (in the workshop) preparing for a high status position. To their friends and to themselves, parents can refer to their children as students rather than as, say, dishwashers. The result is that most workshops for the retarded are fearful of taking complex subcontracts and setting sharp limitations on the vocational development of the clients. While understandable in view of the limited capabilities of the clients, it has made for a situation in which the real potential of many retarded workers has not unfolded. Keeping the subcontract simple in order to accommodate whole groups of retarded workers inevitably traps some individuals whose potentials are higher.

Turning now to still another type of workshop—the workshop for the blind—we find a setting created primarily for long-term, extended employment. In most states, special federal and state wage subsidies build a floor under wages for blind workers. In addition, workshops for the blind can bid for subcontracts under a special act of legislation, the Wagner-O'Day Act, which gives them a privileged position in competing for federal contracts. Consequently, most workshops for the blind have been able to participate in federal contracts. Their situation tends to develop a high gross dollar volume of business in comparison to that of other workshops. The bulk of their business is in manufacturing and producing a finished product, rather than just in selling labor power as is done in subcontract shops. Like the salvage workshops and the workshops for the retarded, those for the blind have not stressed rehabilitation or placement in competitive industry. Some of the large workshops for the blind have begun to emphasize the placement function, but the general picture with regard to rehabilitation of the blind has not changed much over the years.

An important and innovative approach is that developed by the Jewish Vocational Services throughout the country: short-term, transitional workshops designed to help people become employable in a relatively short period of time by focusing on work adjustment techniques. The prototype for this kind of workshop was developed in Chicago under the direction of Gellman and his colleagues (1957). These workshops have developed excellent techniques of work adjustment and have focused on behavioral change as the main goal of the workshop. However, they leave unsolved major problems for the long-term client whose disability is such that he does not become employable as a result of a short-term exposure to these techniques. Then, too, they do not develop a great variety of work experiences since their main emphasis is on changing attitudes and behaviors. They reason that staff attention should be centered on the client rather than on machines or production techniques.

While these approaches are extremely effective, they do not include the long-term disabled person who needs these techniques of work adjustment perhaps even more than do the clients who now receive them.

Working with long-term disabled workers has long been a sore point in the workshop field. Since fee payments usually can be had only for relatively short-term clients, workshops generally do not take on people for whom there is no fee support on a long-term basis. Along with not bringing a fee, many long-term clients are less productive than short-term clients and therefore represent a greater economic deficit for the workshop.

There are problems from the long-term worker's point of view, too. The longer he is in a workshop, the more convinced he becomes that it is a job. It is difficult for him to understand why he is not receiving better pay, sick leave, paid vacations, group insurance benefits, and so on. In short, he wants all of the job rights which he sees other workers achieving. The fact that he is less productive than others does not seem meaningful to him because he is trying just as hard as others who are employed in industry. Because he is not as fast or as productive as others, the long-term worker tends to feel that he is being punished for his disability. Yet, there is little that can be done for him economically in light of DVR's emphasis upon competitive employment and the minimal funding available for permanent or long-term employment in workshops. Another snag: because the long-term client requires time, money, and intensive work, he tends to be bypassed in favor of the short-term client. Thus, the long-term client is denied the benefits of good work adjustment techniques. He gets less supervision and rehabilitation attention than he needs, which, in turn, reinforces a longer stay in the workshop and is a needlessly self-defeating experience for both the client and the workshop. Experience shows that while some chronic and severely ill psychiatric patients need permanent sheltered employment, others, given the opportunity, after one or two years in a workshop stressing work adjustment techniques can move on to competitive employment. A graphic example of the problem is the plight of the person who leaves a mental hospital.

If he is retarded or cerebral palsied or blind, there are long-term solutions available to him through the Association for Retarded Children, United Cerebral Palsy, or Lighthouse for the Blind. If, however, he leaves a mental hospital and is unable to become competitively employable in a short-term evaluation sponsored by the DVR, there is often no long-term resource available. Frequently, such people go back to a mental hospital, not because they are mentally ill again but because the community has not been able to provide a work base as a stabilizer.

Should subcontract sheltered workshops be established in state hospitals? There is a simple but effective alternative: using the routine work necessary to run the hospital to help patients learn to adjust to work. There is nothing new in this concept—the practice of putting patients to work in state hospitals has long been called industrial therapy. But the potential for rehabilitation in this arrangement has seldom been realized.

In the middle 1960's a highly significant demonstration project was conducted jointly by Camarillo (California) State Hospital and the Jewish Vocational Service of Los Angeles (Goertzel, 1965). An existing hospital industry, the bakery, was converted into an effective transitional work adjustment center without establishing a workshop dependent on outside contracts. This project was also noteworthy in that it began vocational rehabilitation earlier than usual within the state hospital and continued it without interruption in the community, it was a joint effort by a large public institution and a community agency, and it helped patients make the transition from hospital to community vocational rehabilitation services with minimum attrition.

The bakery in the state hospital was utilized for the first phase of the rehabilitation effort. The hospital work setting was modified by instituting realistic work demands, introducing a counselor to help patients cope with these demands, and making efforts to change the way in which regular bakery employees used patient helpers. The emphasis in the bakery shifted from simply providing a service to the hospital to rehabilitation of the patients. Handcraft Industries, a unit of the Jewish Vocational Service of Los Angeles,

85

is a well developed transitional work adjustment workshop in Hollywood and was used for the community phase of the vocational rehabilitation effort.

When sheltered workshops began to direct their efforts toward serving the mentally ill, many reported difficulty in getting patients leaving mental hospitals to accept their services. For example, only twelve out of forty-one patients referred by Rockland State Hospital to Altro workshops in New York City actually entered the Altro program (Meyer and Borgatta, 1959). It was concluded that it is too late to offer rehabilitation services after the patient has been discharged. The Camarillo-Jewish Vocational Service project took a number of steps to assure greater acceptance of post-hospital rehabilitation services. In the screening of patients three elements were presented as a continuum: the hospital bakery, the community sheltered workshop, and regular employment. There was only one intake, at which the three steps were presented as a package deal. The community workshop staff sometimes participated in the intake, but regardless of their participation they agreed to accept all patients who completed the bakery phase of the program.

The importance of continuing the program after discharge from the hospital by entering the community workshop phase was stressed to the patients during individual and group counseling sessions. An initial visit, early in the bakery phase, was made to the community workshop so that the patient could have firsthand knowledge of the setting he would enter if successful in the bakery. The patient saw the kind of work he would be performing and, perhaps even more importantly, talked with some of his former fellow hospital patients at the workshop. A second visit was made shortly before the patient was ready to leave the hospital.

During the patient's hospital bakery experience, community workshop staff members visited the bakery and talked with him. These visits were an additional way of making the next step real to the patient and gave him an opportunity to know some of the people who would be supervising his work.

The phase involving the transition from hospital industry to

86

community workshop was completely successful; every patient who completed the bakery phase during the first project year actually entered the community workshop program. This program, then, demonstrated that a major problem in rehabilitation could be solved, for it bridged the gap between hospital and community vocational services.

Future of Workshops

The work flow crisis is not recognized as such nationally, but it should be as it lies at the core of many rehabilitation and financial problems of the workshop movement. It is particularly important because we are on the threshold of sweeping changes in the welfare structure aimed at helping people move from public assistance to a measure of independence through work. Such efforts could be of major significance to the future development of the workshop.

As we have already mentioned, most of the workshops in the country depend upon subcontracts as the major source of work. Even salvage operations such as Goodwill Industries incorporate subcontract shops. The majority of workshops do not experience a consistent flow of work at competitive prices. The lack of a flow of work erodes the rehabilitation process. An appropriate psychological climate cannot be created when workshop clients must stretch work, nor can we simulate a realistic work environment and give an accurate evaluation of the client's potential if the workshop has no real work, no equipment, and inadequate layouts. We cannot fulfill rehabilitation needs when there is not enough work or when the work is not competitively priced. In such cases, the workshop shares the consequences of insufficient and irregular work flow with the client.

The economic consequences of an inadequate supply of work can be disastrous. In slack periods, lack of income raises costs per client, which prevents the workshop from adding additional services, equipment, and production personnel. Also, the workshop is at the mercy of marginal producers who constantly look for bargains in

87

labor. To the extent that the workshop permits itself to be victimized, it offers advantages to the unscrupulous producers as opposed to those who do not attempt to exploit the workshop for cheap labor. Providing cheap labor has also made workshops unpopular with the labor movement which, of course, fears competition from unorganized workers. In periods of economic decline, work that was previously permitted to be subcontracted might as the result of union pressure be prevented from leaving the plant. Union pressure has not been a serious problem in the past since most of the work subcontracted out has not been considered desirable by the organized workers in the plant; it is work that is considered boring, monotonous, and menial or, from the employer's standpoint, too far beneath the skill level of his highly paid employees. In a recession, however, this situation could change.

More serious even than the damaging labor relationships, in my view, is the fact that the workshops fail in their rehabilitation obligations to the clients and to the community when there is not enough work and when the work is not competitively priced.

The picture is not totally grim, however. Legislation has provided considerable sums of money for land purchase, for construction, and for equipping, staffing, and for consultation to individual workshops. Despite these improvements, clients cannot be served properly unless there is an expansion of the work flow.

Basically, there must be a national solution if workshops are to be effective in providing appropriate work at wages that do not demean or exploit the client. Conley's previously cited criticism of the workshop (1965) indicates that the best solution might be to encourage the development of sheltered employment in industry. This would represent a tremendous advance over our current situation, and it is a solution which should be pushed vigorously at national levels. It would certainly require basic legislation, possibly to provide tax advantages for companies which establish sheltered employment facilities or possibly to impose involuntary systems upon industry, which does not voluntarily hire handicapped people in significant numbers. Another solution is to provide funds for the purchase of ongoing existing businesses by rehabilitation agencies and to incorporate handicapped people into these businesses rather than start workshops.

In the long run, government may have to take on more responsibility or even become a guarantor of last resort in the entire field of employment. At this writing, it does not appear that the federal government is likely to move toward large-scale hiring of people with physical and psychological difficulties, even though it has in some departments made such employment more available. The government is likely to intensify its efforts to encourage private business to expand employment for the disabled and disadvantaged. Another solution is for the government to send large amounts of work into workshops as a means of sustaining the work flow and employing many more people than are currently working. If the federal government takes seriously its goal of full employment, it may ultimately have to become a direct employer of disabled and disadvantaged people (Dumont, 1970) as well as an indirect one through subcontracting with workshops.

Is the workshop really capable of a more sophisticated level of work or of handling a greater volume of work than it does? We strongly believe the workshop can. Manpower programs have shown that there are millions of potential clients for workshops. There are marginal people everywhere who, given the opportunity, could benefit from a workshop experience. Although at least half of these people may not be employable in the competitive labor market, they would be highly productive in a workshop or other sheltered employment.

Pilot studies such as those conducted in the Wisconsin (Wood County Project), New Jersey, and New Mexico welfare systems (Wright, Reagles, and Butler, 1969) show that the majority of nondisabled people on public assistance readily welcome the opportunity to work. Many make successful adjustments to competitive work. There is every reason to believe that workshops could become an effective device in such a process. Since programs involving arrangements between government and industry absorb only a small fraction of the disabled and disadvantaged population, the need for workshops is urgent in this area.

89

Rehabilitation in Community Mental Health

With respect to technical readiness to undertake a large flow of work, we submit that it cannot be tested until workshops are presented with a much greater flow of work than they currently handle. Many of our training experiences have convinced us that it is completely ineffective to teach workshops how to become better producers when they are forced to stretch work. Only when they have a large flow of work are they forced to develop techniques of work improvement and full utilization of worker energies. The point is that, given a large enough flow of work, workshops could become socially useful to a million people a year rather than the two hundred thousand or so that now find their way for a period of time into a workshop.

If workshop wages are low, can workshops attract unemployed marginal people who still see themselves as a part of the regular labor force? Workshop wages are certainly unattractive if we look at those for the seriously retarded or others whose disabilities render them ineffectual as producers. But there are many workshops in which the level of technology is considerably higher and where the wage paid approaches the national minimum wage. Then, too, the wage level generally could come close to the national minimum wage if workshops were able to receive good work at fair prices and in sufficient quantity. If we go a step farther, and guarantee people in workshops the minimum wage, we would break the final barrier which prevents many people from taking advantage of what the workshop has to offer.

The manpower situation could be drastically improved if the government recognized the importance of putting people to work and guaranteeing a minimum wage. In actual policy, the nation has moved in this direction, largely through purchasing jobs in industry. Such a program, though effective, has not been able to serve a significant number of people. It is clear that workshops could become the basic social tool for employment—a guaranteed work situation—particularly if the workshop were linked with the welfare system in such a way as to guarantee the minimum wage.

The implications of a guaranteed work situation toward rehabilitation cannot be overlooked. If in our culture employment is the stabilizing force, as we have assumed it is, then it is clear that for many people who have been in mental hospitals a stable work base, guaranteeing a meaningful activity and a minimum income under conditions which are not demeaning, offers great possibilities for genuine recovery. The workshop is just such a setting.

CHAPTER **5**

Sheltered Work Placements

H. Richard Lamb, Cecile Mackota

❊〰❊〰❊〰❊〰❊〰❊〰❊〰❊〰❊〰❊〰❊〰❊

T here are endless opportunities to be creative and innovative in the field of rehabilitation. Nowhere is this more true than in the area of sheltered placement in business, industry, and government; this chapter describes some of these ways of helping the mentally ill maximize their work potential. There is no one right or best way; the particular problems of the clients, the nature of the agency, the lifestyle of its personnel, and the character of the industrial community combine to determine what programs are feasible, desirable, and effective in a community. Some of the programs we describe can be adopted by a rehabilitation agency with very little modification. Others may present ideas which a particular agency cannot directly apply in a practical way. In such instances this chapter may serve as a jumping off place; applicable concepts may be modified and used to pave the way for yet other innovative programs.

In particular, new programs are needed to serve the chronically ill and severely disabled. Generally considered to have low vocational potential, these persons all too often become permanent workshop clients. It is a self-fulfilling prophecy; rehabilitation professionals see many chronic patients as having little potential, devote less time and effort to them, and as a result obtain low vocational performance. With the introduction of less traditional methods, many long-term psychiatric patients can realize their full potential in the world of work.

Work Experience and On-the-Job Training

One way of increasing the likelihood of success of an expatient's transition to competitive employment is a program often referred to as work experience. Such programs have been in existence in San Mateo County (California), and elsewhere, for a number of years with very good results. A work experience program is transitional, generally short-term, and is for people close to being ready for full-time employment. It provides a step between sheltered and competitive employment. Usually it is used with clients with a marketable skill who are not quite ready to tolerate the pressures of competitive employment. It provides a real work environment in which the client can practice his particular skill by placing him in a job similar to what he is going to be doing when he is employed. Work experience placements help clients build confidence and give them a true demonstration of their ability to cope. They acquire the feeling that they are good enough for someone to hire them. A frequently expressed sentiment is, "If I can do it here, I can do it anywhere else."

The San Mateo County Vocational Rehabilitation Service provides such placements in its own county government departments (Lamb and Mackota, 1969). There are obvious advantages to such placements if the rehabilitation agency is part of a govern-

93

ment program. Government services run the gamut of needed work experience placements: janitorial, maintenance, clerical, data processing, hospital work, diet kitchen and cafeteria work, laboratory work, gardening and engineering. Another advantage is that agency-employer relationships are already formed and cooperative working routines are already established, so placements are easier to arrange. Rehabilitation counselors are known to the other departments and can be reached easily for consultation, advice, and support. If the rehabilitation agency is not part of the government, it can still approach industry, government, and social agencies and institutions for such work experience placements. The placements may, of course, be somewhat difficult to find, but as we see in similar programs, such as Fountain House and Thresholds, workable arrangements can be made.

The work experience placement is sheltered in that it is not a regular job. If the client does not work out on the placement, he may be moved to a more suitable placement or back to the workshop, but he does not face the possibility of being fired. The worker also maintains a close link with the rehabilitation counselor. In all other aspects, however, the placement is the same as regular work. It is stressed to both client and supervisor that the client must observe the demands of the job, as he would if he were a civil service employee. He must be punctual, produce good quality work, follow instructions and rules, and work with the other employees of the department. In the event of infractions, he is subject to the same treatment as the other employees, short of being fired. During the entire period, aware of the stress to the client, the counselor is readily available for help in dealing with problems that arise.

Sometimes work experience is used for purposes other than transition to employment. For instance, a work experience placement can be used to lower goals: A woman wants to be a nurse but is not emotionally or intellectually capable. Putting this woman in a nursing placement may help her to see that she is not suited for the work. Or perhaps the counselor is uncertain as to whether a person should work alone or in a group setting. Putting this person in a library placement where he is working alone, returning books to the shelves in a quiet environment, can give important information to both the client and the counselor.

An incidental benefit of these placements is the fact that they serve to educate supervisors, who often have stereotyped concepts of the mentally ill. They discover that patients with emotional problems are like anyone else. They learn that patients can be good workers. Many work experience clients have gone on to civil service jobs, having been recommended by their placement supervisors.

On-the-job training differs from work experience in that the latter is used for clients who have the skill and are lacking mainly in confidence. On-the-job training offers *specific skill training*. An agreement is made between the rehabilitation agency and the employer that the employer will set up a training program. It is generally not transitional. In the majority of cases, the client is trained for the work he is going to do with that employer.

On-the-job training works best when there are funds available to the rehabilitation agency—for example, the state departments of vocational rehabilitation (DVR) theoretically can pay the client a minimum wage and also pay the employer a training fee. In actual practice, DVR and the employer often negotiate and reach an agreement where, for instance, the employer agrees to pay the client and DVR agrees to pay the training fee.

Beyond the Workshop

The most difficult people to move out of a sheltered workshop are the severely and chronically mentally ill, who, under the usual circumstances, easily become permanent workshop clients. These are the people who are most in need of creative techniques to help them move into normal working patterns.

Two sheltered placement methods which may be used for such a client are crew placement and individual placement in industry. Like other vocational placements, they are most effective when the client is paid. Both methods utilize staff members of the rehabilitation agency.

The crew (or group) placement is a safe entry into the real

world of work. It may be either transitional or an extension of the workshop. It involves taking clients in a group to a work placement with a staff member to train and supervise them. There are many variations. The group may work in an industrial plant to fulfill a subcontract, or it may go out as a janitorial service or as a painting crew. Fountain House has a crew that does dishwashing for a factory cafeteria. Other examples of crew placements are described in the sections on Fountain House and the Menlo Park Veterans' Administration Program.

The crew placement is a first step outside of the sheltered setting and gives the clients a glimpse of competitive employment. They see that they are not as different from others as they had imagined. Persons who need group support to work outside the sheltered workshop environment are selected for crew jobs. These clients would be unable, in most instances, to tolerate individual placement. With the backing of the group and the staff member, they are able to go into industry and to be productive. Some of the clients go on to less sheltered employment; others return to the workshop when the crew job is completed.

Crew jobs also influence other clients in the workshop. Those left behind see their co-workers leave and cope successfully with work outside the shop. They begin to feel that a crew placement and, indeed, work in the outside world may be a possibility for them.

Individual Placement

Individual placement, both transitional and permanent, with staff support serves as another avenue out of the workshop. One of the earliest of the innovative programs in the area of sheltered employment for ex-mental patients was begun at Fountain House in New York City (Beard, Schmidt, and Smith, 1963, 1964; Schmidt, Nessel, and Malamud, 1969). Within Fountain House itself are two well-functioning rehabilitation programs. The first is a social and recreational program, offered in the evenings and on weekends, designed to help the members (as the persons served are called) of Fountain House rebuild their confidence, self-esteem, and social skills.

Sheltered Work Placements

The classes and activities range from discussion groups, typing classes, and lectures to arts and crafts, choral singing, and dramatics. The second program utilizes the day-time hours at Fountain House to establish and strengthen primary work habits and motivation for productive work, employment, and eventual financial independence.

Four activity areas constitute this vocationally oriented day program, each of which relates to an essential function of the House: (1) preparation and serving of meals in the cafeteria; (2) housekeeping and janitorial services for the House; (3) office and clerical jobs; and (4) painting and minor repairs in the House. Volunteers, staff, and members work side by side. Fountain House believes that the participation of staff stimulates, encourages, and makes possible the member's participation; in this way the member develops more appropriate work habits, increases his ability to get along with others, and strengthens his motivation for future employment. This belief in the importance of staff doing the same tasks as the members of Fountain House is carried over into the philosophy of the transitional employment program.

The transitional employment program is a stepping-stone for those members who are ready to leave the day program within Fountain House but are not yet ready to go directly into competitive employment. Members are placed individually in jobs in business and industry. These jobs are obtained and supervised by Fountain House staff. Members are paid the regular rate of pay for hours worked. In keeping with the goal of transitional placements, members do not remain on any one placement for more than three or four months. Transitional placement outside of Fountain House in commerce and industry enables the member to assume employment responsibilities gradually, ultimately achieving full-time employment as confidence and capacity are developed. This transitional program is especially well suited for ex-mental patients who, even though they have achieved a good adjustment in the inhouse work setting, are severely threatened by abrupt separation from the sheltered rehabilitation environment of Fountain House.

It should be emphasized that all placements are truly transitional. There is an agreement beforehand that the member is to move on to another placement, or to regular paid employment if he is ready for it, even if the person placed in the job does well, wants to work where he is, and is wanted permanently in the job by the employer. This does not, of course, stop the employer from hiring the member for another position in his organization, so long as the original position remains a transitional one for other placements.

Usually the member is placed where the job requirements are less than his actual capabilities. The intent? So that he can concentrate on demonstrating good work habits, increasing his capacity to perform productive work, and learning to get along with fellow employees. The major emphasis is the resolution of problems in personal adjustment which affect the member's vocational functioning. Because he has skills greater than those required on the job, he is able to focus on problems of personal adjustment at work rather than on the pressure of the work itself.

The member need not start a placement on a full-time basis. A frequent arrangement is for one person to be on a transitional placement in the morning with a second person assuming the same duties in the afternoon. Time is gradually increased until one member is handling the transitional job full time.

When a new placement is found by Fountain House, a staff member goes out and works on the job for anywhere from a few hours to a day or two. In doing this, the staff member gets a first-hand picture of the requirements and pressures of the job, which puts him in a better position to supervise the ex-mental patient when he arrives on the placement. Further, the staff member develops rapport with the employees with whom the patient member is to work. This is important because, in various ways, fellow employees join the rehabilitative effort. Supervisors take pains to help members get oriented and adjusted to the job. Members are included in coffee breaks and receive invaluable support from fellow employees, who frequently take a keen interest in the progress of the member.

An evening meeting is held each week, at Fountain House,

for all members working on transitional placements. Every member gives a brief report of his current placement experience. Problems are brought up and discussed. Members are supportive but at the same time direct; they may, for instance, point out a difficulty that is related not to the job but to a member's own problems.

Many employers are quite receptive to the idea of a placement in their organization, especially if the advantages from a business point of view are clearly pointed out. In general, job placements given to Fountain House solve a number of problems for the employer: Absenteeism is reduced; job performance is usually equal to that normally experienced by the employer, if not superior. Fountain House assumes the training or orientation responsibility when placing a new member, thereby relieving the employer of this task. Then, too, if any problem arises on the job, Fountain House staff are readily accessible. Thus, the employer sees that having a transitional placement in his office or plant is not just a philanthropic gesture, it is good business.

Participating employers attend approximately three meetings a year, usually held at Fountain House in the early evening. Prospective employers also are invited. At these meetings, employers learn more about the placement program and its specific role in the rehabilitation process. Increased understanding of the project by employers does much to maintain their interest and support.

This is an impressive program, but we feel it needs to be qualified in one important respect: We question the concept of individual *transitional* placement for chronically and severely mentally ill patients. In fact, Fountain House has found that a number of their chronic patients go from one transitional placement to another but are never able to go beyond these and adjust to a full-time competitive nonsheltered job. In our opinion, it is asking too much of this particular group of patients repeatedly to make adjustments to different environments and people.

We feel that if chronically and severely mentally ill clients are to be moved out of the workshop, their placement must be understood from the beginning as a permanent one rather than a

99

transitional one; it is to be the client's permanent job. Low-level jobs with a high turnover rate and requiring low skills are best suited for this purpose—for example, locker room attendant at a country club, kennel boy at a veterinary hospital, stock boy in a shoe store, and so on. These jobs are plentiful we find. Opportunities are not really so limited that they need to be reserved for repeated use—an argument sometimes given for keeping placements transitional.

In our work with these chronic patients in the San Mateo County Vocational Rehabilitation Service, counselors solicit employers for jobs, asking that the jobs be given indefinitely to the agency. The agency agrees to select the employee, train him, and supervise him. The agency further agrees to take the responsibility for seeing that the job is done, even if staff has to pitch in at times to do the work. This guarantees to the employer that he will no longer be plagued by absenteeism and turnover. The advantage to the client is that he does not have to go through the usual interviewing process; he is trained by someone he knows and trusts; and he does not have the full responsibility for the job until he is ready to take it.

Initially, a staff member goes to the job with the client and works with him full time. Gradually, over a period of several weeks, the staff member cuts down his time until he is only dropping in for brief periods several times a week, then once a week. Eventually, the client establishes a relationship with his boss or supervisor and is able to function more independently. In most cases, for the really chronic patient it is necessary to continue the weekly visit indefinitely, even if the client seems stabilized. These severely disabled clients, in our experience, need the continuing support of the agency if they are to function successfully. When these brief weekly visits have been discontinued, some clients have experienced a setback which resulted in their being fired from the job. Our experience demonstrates that we must expect to offer extended service to this group of people.

It is apparent that the individual placement program is very consuming of staff time. However, the field of rehabilitation has had little success in returning the truly chronically ill members of our population to employment, and we feel that the investment of staff time is a worthwhile one.

A unique feature of Fountain House is its group placement program, designed for members ready for transitional employment but not yet able to work on an outside transitional placement by themselves, separated from staff and members. These group placements include factory assembly work, two cafeteria and restaurant settings, and work in the warehouse of a national merchandising concern. In each of these settings, from six to ten members work together, with Fountain House assuming responsibility for selection of members assigned to each group. An example of an extremely innovative way in which this program has been implemented is the group placement at a Chock Full O'Nuts restaurant (Schmidt, Nessel, and Malamud, 1969):

On Seventh Avenue in the midtown area of Manhattan our members and staff have assumed total responsibility for the operation of this counter restaurant which serves thousands of customers during each business day and on Saturdays. The operation of the Chock Full store as a rehabilitation project of Fountain House is of special interest because our staff have assumed full responsibility for its day-to-day management. We receive payment from the store for such managerial services. Over a period of a year the store normally spends close to $50,000 in the form of wages and this amount is available to Fountain House members who fill positions. Normally twelve to fourteen employees work in the store. This means that over twenty members can work there on a part-time basis. Almost all positions are filled by our members, with the exception of two employees who have worked there for some years and are not only interested in our project but are extremely helpful in facilitating the work adjustment of our members. Members perform all of the tasks in the store and the placement relates closely to the snack bar on

101

the fifth floor of Fountain House, where members can acquire ex-perience similar to the work which must be performed in the store.

The Thresholds Transitional Placement Program

The Thresholds Transitional Job Placement Program (Dincin and Swift, 1967) is to some extent modeled after that of Fountain House, though with a number of important innovations. As at Fountain House, members are first assigned to work crews doing tasks essential to the maintenance of the Thresholds building or its program, such as routine cleanup, renovation, preparation of the noon meal, shopping, or clerical or switchboard work. There is an active group program which includes a vocational skills group. These didactic and activity-oriented groups are designed to help members handle the basic requirements of finding and keeping a job—that is, how to fill out job applications, how to conduct oneself in the job interview, what employers expect of employees on the job, and how to get along with fellow employees. Role-playing techniques are also used to help members develop these skills. (Thresholds also has an extensive social rehabilitation program, as described in Chapter Seven.) The goal of the work crews is to develop and maintain appropriate work habits to get along with other workers. Regularly scheduled group meetings are held to discuss work assignments, mutual problems, and plans. Staff work alongside members, to provide a work model and to get first hand knowledge of how each person is functioning.

For those members ready to go beyond the work crews in Thresholds itself there are three types of individual transitional job placements in businesses, factories, and other social agencies in the community. (There are also group job placements similar to those described earlier in this chapter.) Each type has its advantages at various stages of recovery and work readiness of the members.

In the first of the individual transitional placements, the Thresholds Paid Placement, a member is expected to have some capacity for productive work, be appropriate in appearance, and have a workmanlike attitude. The hours are flexible, generally ranging from two hours per week to a maximum of twenty hours per week. The member is paid $1.00 an hour by Thresholds; the employer pays nothing. The employer feels he is getting help without paying for it and tends to be flexible in his handling of the member and amenable to suggestions from the agency. The fact that the employer is not paying a regular wage frees both member and employer from some of the pressure which might be present were the productivity of the members an issue of concern. When the member has worked for a while, the employer usually feels uncomfortable about the lack of remuneration and begins to pay something for the work done.

This type of placement calls for close cooperation between the counselor and the employer and intensive work with the member. The amount of counseling required is especially great during the period just prior to, during, and just after the transitional placement has been made. This period of from two to six weeks proves to be the most anxiety-provoking and traumatic for the member. During this period many members are seen in interviews daily and there may be frequent phone calls. The counselor often accompanies the member to his employment interview and occasionally goes with him to work during the first week on the job.

In the Employer-Thresholds Shared Pay Plan, more expectations are made of a member's performance on a job. Thresholds develops a sliding wage scale, with an employer paying part and the agency paying the rest of an hourly wage. As the worker increases his productivity and proves his ability, the employer pays an increasing share of the salary. These jobs are set up at a minimum of four hours per week and range up to twenty hours per week. Thresholds has less control over the placement, and productivity expectations are greater.

The Employer Paid Placements are part-time jobs for which the employer alone pays a going wage rate. More is expected of the employee and as little distinction as possible is made between the member and any other regular employee. These jobs range from ten to thirty-five hours per week.

Although Thresholds believes it is sound practice, staff limitations preclude staff working on jobs prior to placement, as is done at Fountain House.

Thresholds has found repeatedly that members tend to fail when they no longer receive support from the agency. Therefore, members on any of the three types of job placements are required to remain in close contact with Thresholds on a regular basis. Should they not do so, they are taken off the placement. The limitation of twenty hours per week on the first two types of job placements is so that members can participate in other aspects of the rehabilitation program at Thresholds. There is also a job placement meeting which is held once a week for one hour in the evening. All members on placement are required to attend this meeting, where they discuss such topics as job relationships, work attitudes, promptness, initiative, attitudes toward supervision, and inappropriate behavior.

Thresholds assigns one worker to seek and supervise job placements. He regularly contacts and visits each placement and talks with the members on the job. He hears firsthand from the supervisor how the member is doing and relays this information to the member's regular worker at Thresholds. Coordination between the employer and the Thresholds counselor often circumvents potential problems before they have a chance to develop.

The Thresholds staff feels that a key factor in the success of all of their placements, whether in large, medium sized, or small firms, is the fact that one person from the placement itself, usually at the level of foreman, has primary supervisory responsibility for the member and is with him for the bulk of his work time. This makes for a consistency and stability of relationship, with work assignments, demands, and expectations being clearly and consistently defined. It is important, especially initially, that this supervisory individual has the power to control the workload of the member and, perhaps of greater importance, the quality and quantity of closeness that other employees exert upon the member. Thus, the supervisor is in a position to create optimal conditions for a potentially successful work experience.

Contacts made at the top management level, which initially

seemed the most promising, have proven to be less fruitful than contacts with foremen. In a large firm the top management person making the decision to take on the transitional placement is often not involved in the work itself. This was stated clearly to Thresholds by the personnel director of a large firm who said that, while he could arrange to accept a placement, he could not supervise or control the placements since he had no effective control over the "firing line" personnel—for example, the foreman. The foreman, with his mandate to keep company rules and meet productivity requirements, is not in a position to take on an irregular, initially unproductive employee. His lack of involvement and possible animosity if the placement is forced upon him almost always cause the placement to fail. This is not to say that top management support is not crucial. Rather, top management involvement is but a first step; there must also be direct involvement with the member's immediate supervisor.

There is no fixed duration for job placements; the average stay is from five to nine months. It is often hard for a member to move from a familiar placement to a new situation which is more demanding. A constant attempt is made, however, to adhere to the concept of transition and reinforce the expectation of movement to the members.

Thresholds recognizes that many members require long-term emotional support even after they have been successfully placed in a permanent job. The doors of the agency remain open to the member even though he might be officially terminated. This must be emphasized and reemphasized to staff, for there is a tendency on the part of the worker to let go too precipitously because he feels that he has accomplished his task when the member appears securely placed on a job.

An Innovative Hospital Sheltered Workshop

The Menlo Park (California) Veterans' Administration Hospital Program began in 1957 with the establishment within the hospital of a sheltered workshop. It is a nonprofit organization governed by a board of directors made up of interested private citizens in the community and professionals on the hospital staff (McDonough, 1969). The hospital supplies space and minimum personnel (a psychologist with a Ph.D. degree who serves as the workshop director and two shop foremen with experience as psychiatric aides). Other support and financing come entirely from funds earned in the production of goods and services by the workshop.

This workshop has reached beyond the hospital walls to become involved in projects in the community which provide sheltered, paid work opportunities both for patients in the hospital and for patients discharged from the hospital. A notably successful enterprise has been the taking over of a gasoline service station across the street from the hospital. Seven patients are employed full time at the station and receive training in a number of tasks suited to their individual capacities. Services include the usual mechanical work, lubrication, carwashing, and the like. A number of patients placed at the station have gone on to competitive employment at other service stations. The hospital gives effective help to the enterprise by having much of the work needed for maintenance of hospital vehicles done at the workshop-operated station.

A second off-the-grounds project involves the restoration of single family homes which have been abandoned by the owner and have reverted to the original financing agency. Many of these properties are in need of extensive renovation and rebuilding. The workshop enters into a contract to rehabilitate a property, and crews of patients, operating out of workshop-owned vehicles, prepare it for resale. Tasks include plastering, painting, carpentry and floor tiling, in addition to the reconditioning of the grounds and landscaping. The director of this program concludes that "the traditional hospital-based sheltered workshop, when operated as a nonprofit corporation, is especially well suited to the employment of mental patients in workshop-owned enterprises outside the hospital walls."

Fairweather's Sheltered Subsociety

It was noted in Chapter One that a sheltered work situation is only part of the solution for many ex-mental hospital patients.

106

Fairweather et al. (1964, 1969), recognizing the need of the chronic mentally ill for support in many aspects of their lives, developed a sheltered subsociety in the community to meet the housing and social as well as vocational needs of these patients. Carefully designed evaluation was built in to each phase of his program. There was a control group for each group of patients being exposed to his experimental programs, and sophisticated statistical analysis was employed. Thus, it is possible to evaluate in a meaningful way all aspects of his program; from the research point of view Fairweather's program has been a model for experimental social innovation. (See Chapter Eight for a discussion of the research aspects of this program.)

Fairweather began by establishing in the hospital a program centering around the use of small problem-solving groups. It was found that these small groups of patients whose daily activities were organized around solving their own problems could be effective even when they were composed of the most chronic patients. To complete this program successfully, each patient had to progress through four steps of increasing responsibility and rewards—that is, money and passes outside of the hospital. The small group was responsible, as a unit, for each individual's progress through these steps. Although the program was effective in getting patients out of the hospital sooner, the readmission rate was as high for these patients as for those in the control group, who had been exposed to the traditional treatment program of the hospital. The crucial factor in remaining in the community was found to be the amount of support that the patient received from the people with whom he lived. When these facts had become clear, Fairweather's group decided to move these problem-solving patient groups as units from the hospital to the community.

This new phase of the program involved setting up the Community Lodge program: a dormitory where the patients live together, and a sheltered work situation—a janitorial service owned and operated by the expatients themselves.

Initially, those in the Community Lodge program needed considerable supervision, but they eventually were able to handle all of their problems themselves. Medical care was provided by a private physician in the community. All of the expatients' customary daily needs, such as food preparation, were managed by the group itself. Eventually, these ex-mental patients became entirely autonomous and self-supporting. The increase in the number of patients in the Lodge program who were able to remain in the community was striking as compared with patients in the control group who were receiving traditional community services. Furthermore, all patients in the Lodge program were employed, either in the janitorial service or in the necessary functions in the Lodge such as meal preparation. But reduction in recidivism and increased employment were not the only benefits. The members of the Lodge also had strong feelings of pride about the organization, themselves, and their accomplishments.

Fairweather notes a number of points that are crucial to the success of his program. First, a high degree of ego-involvement must be developed by the participants in order to make the subsystem work. The task performed by the members must be meaningful to them and be regarded by them as important. The feeling of identification with the success of the organization is enhanced by the patient's ownership of the business. Further, the subsociety must give as much autonomy to its members as is possible, consistent with their behavioral performance.

Fairweather stresses the need for the emergence of leaders from the patient group itself. In this regard, he found that heterogeneous group composition with a mix of both socially active and passive members creates a social climate which provides an opportunity for leaders to emerge. Homogeneous composition of all socially active or all passive, inactive members produces intergroup conflict, in the former case, and stagnation in the latter.

Maximum efforts are made to organize this newly created social system in such a way that the patient's social status depends not on his psychopathology but on what he is able to or chooses to achieve with the nonimpaired portions of his ego-functioning. Within the subsociety there is a vertical organization so that a division of labor is possible and also a meaningful role can be found for all members. Thus, if upward mobility is permitted, those members motivated and capable of assuming higher social statuses (such as crew foreman for the janitorial service) do so. At the same time a meaningful social position is available to those members who are not capable of or who do not aspire to higher social positions within the organization. If a diversity of types of work is provided within the subsystem, it is more likely that work which has meaning for every member can be found. Thus, in the lodge program there are jobs within the lodge, such as the kitchen crew and the bookkeeper, and jobs in the subsociety business. Within these jobs are different work statuses: foreman and worker. Even within the worker category, it is possible to reward the men monetarily according to their productivity, with the marginal workers getting less than the more productive workers.

Fairweather also stresses establishing internal norms which are tolerant of deviant behavior. At the same time, the group must make it clear to each member that such deviant behavior must be limited as much as possible to the subsystem and must not be manifest in the community at large. Thus, the group may tell a patient that it is acceptable to hallucinate in the lodge, or in the truck going to or from work, but that, out on the job, conversing with the hallucinated voices is not permitted.

Sociologically, this sheltered subsociety gives the chronic patient a social role in the community which is not labeled and stigmatized as deviant; it provides sufficient social distance from community agents of social control so that the chronic deviant's rule-breaking behavior becomes less visible to the community at large. This allows behavior to be controlled and regulated within the framework of the subsociety itself, where there is greater understanding of the problems and where there are therapeutic ways of dealing with them. While social controls are stressed, there is also emphasis on setting up a system which ensures that the patients continue to take their medications. Fairweather does not see his lodge program as transitional. It is a permanent subsociety. He feels that, even for those patients who make a good adjustment in his community program, few would be able to remain in the community if they left the supportive environment of the program.

Involving Industry

There are many advantages in involving industry in rehabilitation programs. A school system, for example, invites industry to use its expertise and personnel to set up in the schools vocational training programs which are relevant to industry's needs in their own factories and offices. The programs are then utilized not just by the schools but by the rehabilitation agencies in the community. Moreover, industry, involved and interested, becomes actively helpful in placement.

The program at the Owens-Illinois Corporation at Toledo, Ohio, illustrates another way that industry can become involved in rehabilitation, in this instance rehabilitation of the socially and culturally disadvantaged. Sponsored by the U.S. Department of Labor (through the National Alliance of Businessmen) this cooperative program aims at giving employment to the hard-core unemployed.

The Owens-Illinois Corporation recognized that the program was doomed to failure without some innovative means of helping such employees solve their problems of orientation to the work culture. These clients had never clearly understood what was expected of them in the world of work. They did not understand the importance placed on punctuality and regular attendance on the job, or that personal business should be attended to outside of work hours; they did not know how to relate to fellow workers, how to respond to supervision, how to budget one's income, or how to deal with creditors.

An executive of the company approached the Rehabilitation Counseling Department of the University of Iowa for help in implementing the program. Arrangements were made for students in the Master's program to do their field placement in Toledo, working with the disadvantaged employees. Because the plan worked so well, Owens-Illinois now has rehabilitation counselors on its permanent staff.

Sheltered Work Placements

In programs such as the one at Owens-Illinois, responsibilities are well defined. The federal government identifies and locates the target population and helps finance the operation by a negotiated contract. Industry agrees to hire, train, and retain those located. Normal qualifications for jobs are waived. Rehabilitation counselors' responsibilities are to identify individual problems and needs, and to provide individual and group counseling and comprehensive services tailored to help with social as well as job-related skills.

Referrals to the company come from Neighborhood Opportunity Centers. Screening is performed by the State Human Resources Development Agency in these ghetto areas. Next, those selected are hired by the company as salaried employees and sent to a central training facility where they receive training for the jobs they are going to do. At the same time, counselors are assigned to them. Intensive counseling is done until the workers are placed in one of the Owens-Illinois plants. Counseling is also available for problems which come up after the placement or for help in upgrading to a higher position.

The counselor in this setting must understand a different culture with its own unique value system:

The counselor is constantly walking on delicate ground when dealing with differences in values. He should always express respect for the client's values, yet try to change those that are destructive. If the counselor can alter the client's concept of survival, somehow establishing that survival by employment is the most rewarding form of self-sufficiency, the client may see the need for rehabilitation more easily. It cannot be overemphasized that usually the client must be willing to adapt or modify certain of his values that serve as deterrents to his eventual employment. But the counselor must revise some of his own values too, and try to understand some of the practices that have proven themselves as survival mechanisms in the ghetto. Because circumstances keep the ghetto man from conventional means of adult pride (supporting his own family, succeeding in business, advancement financially, directing his own future), the

111

black ghetto has formulated different self-images that allow for different definitions and sources of pride (amount of pocket money, sexual exploits, expensive clothes, beating a nonsupport rap, consistent victory in fist fights, athletic contest, gambling). The ghetto man has found antisocial means to maintain his pride. The counselor has only a short time to try to appeal to that pride and rechannel it to the idea of employment as an accomplishment. What does the counselor have to offer his clients in terms of immediate or short-term goals? The black ghetto dweller is typically impatient of long-term goals; he is not satisfied with delayed rewards. The usual rehabilitation program is not designed to give rapid reinforcement. Red tape must be decreased, the purpose of testing, and evaluation must be well understood or not be used at all. Some programs will need to be cut short to adapt to short attention spans; pressures from the ghetto world, from the old pattern of living, are intensified for ghetto clientele, and without immediate rewards the involvement of the client cannot be captured and kept [Townsend, 1970].

But counselors in this program have also found that they are dealing with many of the same work adjustment problems encountered with the physically handicapped and the mentally ill. Techniques of rehabilitation counseling which have proven successful in resolving these problems with the handicapped are also appropriate with the disadvantaged.

The job is more difficult, however, because the counselors are seen by their clients as part of the company power structure by virtue of their having been retained by company management. The counselors are seen as authority figures with considerable influence on whether the worker continues in the job. Trust is, therefore, more difficult to establish. On the whole, however, the counselors are successful in helping workers cope with the many crises and problems which arise in this population as they acclimate themselves to the worker role.

After the first six months of operation, the program at Owens-Illinois showed a success rate of sixty per cent, far higher than that reported by other companies which hired the disadvantaged but did not employ counselors. The Owens-Illinois rate of success is at least equal to the usual assimilation rate into similar jobs for the population at large. What is important about this program of coordinated services is its recognition that the usual method of introducing a new employee to industry (an orientation from the personnel department as to hours, pay, benefits, company rules, and so on) plus training, is not sufficient to result in successful job adjustment of socially disadvantaged employees. Counselors focus on such areas as personal adjustment, interpersonal skills, and attitudes toward work and authority so that the client has more chance of becoming an effective employee and often of improving his functioning in other areas of his life.

A Final Word

We have outlined a number of programs that we consider to be creative. Someday, looking back, they may appear as crude beginnings as we gain more expertise in this complex field of rehabilitation.

In this connection, a note of caution needs to be sounded. In too many instances innovative programs which have excited the imagination of the rehabilitation staff and even gained national attention later became rigid and ceased to develop and grow. The agencies seemed satisfied to rest on their laurels, and needed evaluation of how the programs affected the people they served was not done. Sometimes the staff, with a vested interest in its once innovative program, shifted its energies from evaluation and further development to justification. Thus, paralleling the need to be innovative is the equally important need to be flexible, objective, and critical so that innovation is an ongoing process. The resources of business and industry and the expertise of rehabilitation professionals can be a potent combination for combatting social problems.

CHAPTER 6

Therapeutic Housing

Charles Richmond

❦❦❦❦❦❦❦❦❦❦❦❦❦❦❦❦❦❦❦❦❦❦❦❦❦

Supervised housing has become an essential element of effective rehabilitation of the emotionally disabled. All too often failure to provide suitable supportive living arrangements has caused rehabilitation efforts to founder; supervised housing, if properly utilized, is an integral part of the rehabilitation process. By providing an environment which is free of hospital-type institutionalism but which supports and mobilizes the person's strengths and resources, supervised housing programs foster social reintegration and reinforce other rehabilitation activities. The support and encouragement of staff and other residents in supervised housing facilities can create an atmosphere that bridges the gap between dependence and the development of self-determination and independence.

Residential community care for mentally ill persons has been provided for centuries as an alternative to hospitalization or imprisonment; a well known example is the Gheel Colony in Belgium (Muth, 1961). In this country, the majority of mentally ill persons in supervised community living situations is in boarding and family care homes. But, as we have seen in Chapter One, these living accommodations usually leave much to be desired from the point of view of rehabilitation. In contrast, two relatively new modalities, the halfway house and satellite housing arrangements, can be a vital force for rehabilitation.

Halfway Houses

In 1954 Rutland Corner House in Boston, which had been engaged since 1877 in providing a "protective temporary home for transient and needy women" (Landy and Greenblatt, 1965), shifted to providing a program of transitional aftercare for formerly hospitalized mental patients. This was the first community-based transitional residence or "halfway house" for mentally ill persons in this country. The number of halfway houses for the mentally ill and socially disabled grew slowly but consistently during the 1950's, culminating in a great surge in the late 1960's. This surge probably received its impetus from the mass exodus from state hospitals, the advent of psychotropic drugs, and the development of community mental health concepts. The survey for the Joint Commission on Mental Illness and Health (1961) located only seven halfway houses in 1959, all established since 1954. Now there are more than two hundred halfway houses in the United States. However, because of the endless variety of halfway houses and the lack of a commonly accepted definition of what a halfway house is, it is extremely difficult to determine the exact number of such facilities. There are, for example, houses for formerly hospitalized mental patients, houses for preventing hospitalization, and houses which combine both purposes. There are houses for alcoholics, exconvicts, drug abusers, addicts, adolescents, and the retarded; houses for men, for women, and coed houses; houses in which the transitional period is limited to a few months and others in which it is a year or more.

Rehabilitation approaches vary widely, also. Some halfway

houses are little more than boarding houses, having few or no reha-bilitation goals. Most halfway houses, however, share certain com-mon functions. In addition to providing a place to live, they are transitional, encourage socialization and resocialization, and empha-size vocational rehabilitation and the constructive use of leisure.

The purpose of halfway houses is often misunderstood by the public and by professionals alike who regard them simply as protective and sheltered places to live or as small hospital-like pro-grams in the community where medications are meted out and psychotherapy or other traditional treatment is offered. Halfway houses, however, offer much more than that. They are character-ized by a group living experience which is designed to produce changes in social behavior and in ability to function independently in the community. Referral to a halfway house should be based on the individual's need for such a rehabilitative socialization or reso-cialization experience and not simply on the need for a place to live while the rehabilitation process is carried on elsewhere.

The transitional nature of residence at halfway houses af-firms the expectation that residents are to move toward a more in-dependent existence. How long a resident remains at a halfway house varies depending upon the expectations of each house. Some halfway houses pride themselves on a brief stay of perhaps three to six months, while others consider this period much too brief to ac-complish their aims. The length of stay also depends largely on what the referral source, the halfway house staff, and the patient hope to accomplish. Ordinary living accommodations available in the community also affect the length of stay. Where there is ample housing, such as apartments, residence clubs, and rooming houses, the move to an outside living situation is greatly simplified. Where there is not ample housing, halfway house residents who are ready to move on may remain longer than necessary simply because there is nowhere else to go.

Many houses set a one-year maximum limit on the length of time a resident may remain. A few houses, however, accommodate a small number of residents in excess of two years. They are usually patients for whom independent living in the wider community is not considered a short-term reality. This practice is detrimental both to the "long stay" resident, who by virtue of his special status may cease to strive toward independence, and to the other residents, who receive a double message about how long they really can stay in what is supposed to be a transitional facility. Halfway houses might best maintain a commitment to a relatively short, time-limited service. Since they are difficult to establish, those few that are available should be accessible to as many persons as possible who need the unique services offered. If long-term accommodations are also needed, they should be established as supplements to halfway houses. Satellite housing, to be discussed later, represents an innovative method of providing long-term accommodations to patients who would otherwise remain in halfway houses for inappropriately long periods.

Facilities which set no limits with regard to length of stay are not halfway houses in the strict sense but supervised residences or residence clubs. They, too, can serve the cause of rehabilitation. For instance, Boerum Hill Home for Adults (formerly Cobble Hill Center) in Brooklyn, New York, is an example of a rehabilitation-oriented, long-stay residence. The director of the program states:

Although we are different [from halfway houses] in many respects, there are certainly similarities. Essentially, although our techniques vary, we both endeavor to provide the discharged patient with a supportive social and psychological world that will enable him to function more adequately in the outside world. Basic differences involve our size, period that residents stay with us, and our intimate relationship with a vocational rehabilitation institute that is located on one of the floors of our eight-story residence. We have a capacity of 180 residents who may remain with us, if necessary, for several years rather than months, and we expect that a small group will live out their lives with us. At the beginning we considered Cobble Hill Center to be a halfway house, but the anxiety generated among the residents led us to assure a more flexible approach toward length of stay, and we feel that this has enhanced the rehabilitation process [Personal communication].

Boerum Hill Home is, to be sure, a unique supervised residence, considering the large number of persons accommodated, its rehabilitation focus, and the extensive social and vocational rehabilitation services located within the building. Despite the option for an indeterminate stay, many residents choose to leave after a brief period. The facility, therefore, has made available a number of three- and four-room furnished apartments for residents who have obtained jobs or who do not require the supervision provided at the main residence and wish more independence and autonomy. The individuals living in the apartments may still make use of the Boerum Hill facilities which include an extensive social and recreational program.

Halfway houses draw from a number of treatment modalities, including milieu therapy, the therapeutic community, behavioral modification, and reality therapy. Indeed, there is no universal halfway house treatment model. The one ingredient common to the effective house, however, is the expectation that a resident can and will achieve a higher level of functioning.

The effective halfway house helps residents see themselves as potentially healthy, rather than as sick, individuals. Residents are expected to mobilize their strengths and to realize their full resources and potential. Regressive and bizarre behavior is dealt with on the basis of its effect upon others as well as on the basis of its meaning to the individual. Adult and socially responsible behavior is expected from residents, and opportunities for such behavior are provided within the halfway house. The high expectation halfway house as distinguished from a low expectation or nurturing approach (Wilder, Kessell, and Caulfield, 1968), differentiates the dynamic and successful halfway house from those which are halfway houses in name but in reality resemble boarding homes. The high expectation approach requires both residents and staff to value socially appropriate and productive behavior. Staff members are the key to the communication of this value, for they are the carriers of the high expectation culture. They must believe that there is a higher potential in all human beings and that emotionally or socially handicapped persons are no exception. There are, of course, those disintegrated, fragmented, unmotivated, and hostile persons sometimes referred to halfway houses who severely test such beliefs. If at the outset staff members have major doubts whether such persons can make it, or if they feel that they do not want to work with a particular resident, the staff members must come to grips with their negative bias and make some commitment to finding a way to work with the individual. Otherwise they will have engaged in a self-fulfilling prophecy and the individual *will* fail. This is not to say that simply expecting a resident to succeed will make it so. Our experience shows, however, that once a trusting relationship is established and some basic needs are fulfilled, the majority of these difficult residents will, more often than not, strive to meet at least some of the staff's expectations. This potential for improvement must be emphasized if the halfway house is not to limit its services to a narrow range of "good" residents.

A high expectation philosophy is communicated to residents both verbally and nonverbally. For example, at El Camino House in San Mateo County, California, the physical milieu communicates informality and a homelike atmosphere. Its homey living room, dining room, and recreational space, in addition to the sleeping quarters, appear comfortable and lived in. The social milieu says to the resident, "While here, you are a person not a patient. We are interested in your abilities, your strengths, your talents. We expect you to conduct yourself as any ordinary citizen; usual courtesies and consideration toward others are expected." Individuality, autonomy, and involvement in the house program are highly valued. Deviant behavior is tolerated within limits. Behavior which is overtly self-destructive, destructive toward others, or which infringes on the rights of others is dealt with as unacceptable and irresponsible. Residents are expected to participate actively during the day in some constructive endeavor, whether it be vocational training, school, work, day treatment center, or regularly scheduled volunteer activity (Richmond, 1969). Other expectations are that the resident handle his own prescribed medications, that he arrange his own transportation, and that he participate fully in the cleaning, maintenance, and cooking within the house. The message is that he is capable and that he is able to function in the community or, at least, that he can learn to do so with encouragement and support.

The halfway house is most effective when these expectations are communicated more by peers than by staff—that is, from resident to resident. To facilitate this process at El Camino House, residents have weekly house meetings in which staff are not present. Deviant or unacceptable behavior within the house or the community is recorded by any resident or staff member in an open journal which is kept in the common entry hall. Verbal and written reports of behavior which appears to affect an individual's progress, or which affects the group as a whole, provide the agenda for the house meeting. Staff participates prior to the meeting to provide any additional information the group needs or requests and after the meeting to hear group decisions regarding the items under discussion. Socialization and resocialization, then, are promoted and communicated primarily by the physical and social milieu and by the expectations of both staff and residents.

What we call life habit training is needed by many residents. For instance, some residents may learn to cook for the first time; others may learn how to manage money. In the area of personal hygiene, there may be individual guidance or perhaps classes conducted by volunteers on grooming, beauty tips, or the use of cosmetics. The use of leisure is often a problem. Some houses encourage their residents to use recreational facilities in the community; others provide inhouse and out-of-the-house group recreational activities. Some houses, such as Conard House in San Francisco, have extensive social and recreational activities which serve not only residents of the halfway house but nonresidents as well, usually formerly hospitalized patients living in the community. Conard House accommodates thirty-one residents in the house, but serves more than 250 persons per month in its evening drop in program, which is supervised by a full-time recreational therapist.

Treatment and rehabilitation services may also include formal individual and group counseling within the house, informal guidance in using transportation, shopping, and budgeting, or simple instruction on how to use a dishwasher or a coin operated laundromat.

Readers interested in establishing halfway houses in their communities and in knowing more than has been outlined here of the problems and pitfalls of such a venture are referred to an earlier work by this author (Richmond, 1969).

Vocational Assistance. Work places the individual in a structured social situation and provides an opportunity for conformity to important societal norms. Many halfway houses emphasize vocational assistance as a primary service of the facility, while most others regard helping the resident to find and keep employment as a very important secondary goal. Since halfway houses are designed to assist the reintegration of the patient into the community, they naturally concern themselves with the vocational progress of their residents. While the socialization and resocialization experiences of halfway house residents may enhance the resident's ability to succeed on a job, the halfway house is not a substitute for a sheltered vocational workshop. Halfway houses provide life habit training through resident involvement in activities necessary to the everyday operation of the house such as housework, light maintenance, and cooking. These activities, however, do not prepare residents for most types of jobs available in the community but for the everyday process of caring for themselves and their property.

The role of the halfway house in vocational rehabilitation depends to a great extent upon what other vocational resources are available in the community. When outside vocational counseling or sheltered workshop and employment services exist, such resources should be used. The halfway house attempts to motivate the individual toward constructive use of his time and directs him, when he is ready, toward use of available vocational resources. The house encourages his vocational activity and maintains a liaison with the vocational resource to ensure that the house and the vocational agency do not work at cross purposes. Many houses achieve a very close working relationship with vocational rehabilitation services. Again, using the example of El Camino House, the staff works very closely with the County Vocational Services Center, which provides vocational counseling, sheltered workshop, work experience placement, and referral for more specialized trainiing. A member of the Vocational Services Center staff regularly attends a meeting with halfway house staff to share information and to collaborate on the planning for persons who are clients of both facilities. Throughout, the client-member is actively involved in the planning of his rehabilitation program. Often admission to the halfway house is dependent upon the person's admission into the program of the Vocational Services Center, and the two staffs confer immediately following intake.

In areas where community vocational services are not readily available or accessible, the halfway house often takes on responsibility for vocational planning. Some halfway houses were established expressly to initiate or increase vocational services and work closely with local departments of vocational rehabilitation which fund and sponsor them. Work related activities are built into the structure of the halfway house. For example, a staff member of the halfway house may conduct prevocational and vocational counseling in the house by leading role playing groups related to job interviews or sometimes by assisting the client to find volunteer work, work experience placements, or actual competitive employment.

The Contrast With Boarding Homes

Many models of residential community care are in use today, including family care homes, boarding homes, foster homes, group homes, and halfway houses. Unfortunately, these terms often are used interchangeably so that the distinctions among them are blurred and sometimes confusing. All of these models of residential care, with the exception of halfway houses, operate by accepting into a private home paying guests referred by public social agencies, families, or hospitals. The usual purpose of these homes is to provide long-term care and supervision for those unable to care for themselves. Generally, the patient is supervised by the caretaker, usually the owner of the home, who in turn is provided consultation and supervision by a social worker from a social welfare agency or a hospital.

The term used to describe a particular type of residence, whether it be foster home, boarding home, or family care home, depends either on the definition of the state or local licensing authority, if there is one, or, if the home is not licensed, on the whim of the caretaker-owner. Raush and Raush (1968) point out that

in any city sufficiently large to have a diversity of boarding homes, there will be found a landlady who prides herself in providing some modicum of community life for those difficult and eccentric isolates who might be classified psychiatrically as chronic ambulatory schizophrenics; there probably are other landladies who pride themselves in being able to manage "rough" characters and to keep out of trouble those whom psychiatrists would classify as psychopathic personalities or acting out character neurotics; some landladies, too, pride themselves on reforming alcoholics, or at least in keeping them sober enough to hold down jobs.

Many of these landladies do perform a valuable service to the psychiatrically disabled—that is, they provide shelter, food, and concern. Some boarding home operators regard their residences as halfway houses since this is the term most in vogue at this time. These homes are not halfway houses, however, since they provide no formalized or systematic program of rehabilitation and are not part of a transition to independent living.

Wechsler (1960) points out that an essential feature distinguishing the halfway house from the family care or boarding home is the use of the group as part of the rehabilitation process. The use of milieu therapy, where the group serves as an agent of change, facilitates socialization experiences. According to Wechsler,

The halfway house may be considered to be a sheltered social environment, within which there is a tolerance of behavior which would be considered deviant elsewhere. The resident may be freer to act and to try out new rules and behaviors within this sheltered

setting. However, the resident group may act to modify the individual's behavior to make it conform to group norms. As the individual drops patterns of behavior disapproved of by the group, and adopts behavior which is encouraged, it is hoped that this learning will be generalized to social interaction outside the house. The halfway house resident group thus acts to socialize or resocialize the individual.

Although it is certainly less expensive to maintain a patient in a family care or boarding home than in a hospital, Lamb and Goertzel (1971) question whether these patients, though no longer in the hospital, really are in the community. A custodial posture often predominates in boarding homes, despite efforts to upgrade services and supervision. Such efforts often last only for the duration of a research or demonstration project or during the tenure of a particularly interested and innovative worker. Boarding homes and family care homes often fail in their mission to provide an experience in social living within a family setting. For the most part, docility and passivity are accepted modes of behavior. The relationship between the operator and the patient is similar to that between parents and young children rather than to that between adults. The homes are often far from transportation and not within easy reach of shopping areas and other centers of social life. Little is expected of the resident, and his waking hours are often spent within the home, watching television or just sitting.

Attempts are often made to improve the situation through supervision and consultation. However, even when these efforts fail, the supervising worker is reluctant to stop using the home. Closing the home means loss of a placement resource and the time-consuming transfer of patients to other homes, if there are other homes and if openings are available. Thus, if the caretakers of the home must be released from their obligations, one loses not just the sponsors, but the physical plant as well. Understandably, there is a reluctance to take such action and therefore an accumulation of mediocre caretakers and mediocre homes builds up. Another problem is that boarding home operators are usually paid by the number of persons residing in their homes and not rewarded in any way for efforts toward rehabilitation.

Despite all these problems, exceptions do exist. There are boarding home operators who, on their own or in conjunction with the guest's social worker, do emphasize rehabilitation approaches. Such operators encourage their guests to find sheltered or competitive employment, to increase their social activities, and even encourage movement to more independent living.

New Directions. Although originally designed to assist patients to cope with the arduous transition from confinement in a hospital to life in the community, halfway houses have, from the beginning, accommodated small numbers of persons with no history of hospitalization who needed the halfway house in order to prevent hospitalization and remain in the community. To the extent that the community mental health movement is successful in reducing long periods of hospitalization, the original role of the halfway house may further shift from that of providing a bridge between institution and community to that of serving primarily the acutely disturbed as an alternative to hospitalization.

One example is the Community Care Home, operated by Rehabilitation Mental Health Services, Inc., Santa Clara, California. This program accepts acutely mentally ill individuals who need to be away from a stressful situation and enables them to recover without removal from the community. The facility is used solely as an alternative to hospitalization, providing psychiatric treatment in conjunction with social rehabilitation and vocational services.

The results of a controlled study of the Community Care Home as compared to a state hospital revealed that the facility not only treated patients more effectively but did so in a shorter period of time. Patients treated in the Community Care Home tended toward more active, productive means of dealing with real life problems, suffered fewer relapses, and achieved greater vocational success than did the control group treated at a state hospital. The Community Care Home life management treatment approach was demonstrated to be more practical, more functional, more realistic, and more related to the everyday needs of the patient than the treatment in the state hospital. The research results indicate that treating patients in a community setting may be the treatment of choice for a majority of patients and that community mental health services may have underestimated the potential for successfully treating acutely disturbed patients in an open-door halfway house setting (Goveia and Tutko, 1969).

Those characteristics of the halfway house which distinguish it from the hospital are the essential ingredients of the therapeutic process. The halfway house provides a protective subsociety in a familylike, nonmedical setting. The small group composition, the informal but structured atmosphere, the emphasis upon health rather than illness, and the increased contact with the mainstream of community life create a milieu which cannot readily be duplicated, even in the most progressive and modern open-door hospitals. Halfway houses are not self-contained societies as are most mental hospitals; residents must relate to the community in order to obtain medical care, work, schooling, and recreation.

Sponsors of halfway houses are also becoming increasingly involved in developing residentially oriented services for special problem groups. In response to the paucity of community based open-door services for adolescents, private agencies have initiated transitional residences for that age group. Rehabilitation Mental Health Services, Inc., Santa Clara, California, operates the Adolescent Residential Center, and Mental Health Recovery, Inc., San Mateo, California, recently established Pedregal House for seriously disturbed youngsters between sixteen and nineteen years of age. The Manhattan Project, Los Angeles, California, sponsored by the Salvation Army, consists of four houses for adolescents and young adults and is essentially a resident-run operation. Residential programs for adolescent and young adult drug users and addicts include such diverse programs as the Phoenix Houses, Reality House East, and Daytop Village in New York; Reality House West and Walden House in San Francisco.

Baker Places, Inc., San Francisco, has a young mothers' flat for six single mothers and their babies. The mothers live in cooperative group style. Each woman contributes to the housekeeping, cooking duties, and babysitting. Individual counseling and group meetings are available.

Scattered or Satellite Housing

Raush and Raush (1968) in an excellent study of halfway houses state: "What can be done to serve those residents who may never be able to live independently but who do not require hospital security remains a pressing problem for the halfway house administrator." They suggest planned group discharge of patients from the halfway house to permanent and semicustodial "quarterway houses." They further suggest facilitating transition to the community by a series of graduated steps, possibly joint living arrangements with minimal or no supervision. "A potential network of halfway house, three-quarterway, and quarterway houses," say these authors, "represents an alternative to the mental hospital . . . a network of such houses with opportunity for mobility among them offers a more appropriate structure and far greater opportunities for rehabilitation and reintegration than does the mental hospital." Indeed, over the past five years just such innovative extensions of the halfway house have emerged.

Extramural housing, where patients live in small groups without live-in staff but with supervision, may in fact be considered the current movement in the field. And this movement is not confined to programs serving the psychiatrically disabled. Hawker (1966) writes of a program for alcoholics in England:

Most pressing, perhaps, is [the problem] of what is to happen to men when they eventually leave the house; we suspect, in fact, that some alcoholics may be able to maintain sobriety indefinitely in an atmosphere such as the house provides, but that they would scarcely survive the shock of returning to solitary lodgings. We may, perhaps, establish a series of small local lodging houses for exresidents, with no wardens or staff of any description . . . the exresidents still regard the parental house as the place to which they could drop in during the evenings, and perhaps attend the regular Wednesday evening group sessions.

Numerous graduate residents of Austin McCormack House for exconvicts in San Francisco have tended to settle in apartments in the neighborhood of the house. Staff assists residents in finding housing and provides crisis intervention as necessary. These services did not develop as a planned expansion of program but evolved informally as residents who were enrolled in school desired more privacy for studying and greater autonomy than they had had in the house. A satellite relationship between these former residents and the house developed as the former residents returned to visit the house and use some of its services.

Fountain House, described in Chapter Five, is believed to be the first organization to utilize the concept of supervised semi-independent housing in this country. In 1958 a one-room apartment located directly across the street from Fountain House was leased; by 1971 the project had been expanded to thirty apartments with a total capacity of fifty-nine persons. Fountain House has used apartment living in conjunction with its day and evening social and vocational rehabilitation programs in lieu of establishing a single residental halfway house setting.

The Satellite Housing Program in San Mateo County, California, administered with El Camino House and Pedregal House as Mental Health Recovery, Inc., was initiated primarily because of the lack of adequate economical housing for graduates of El Camino House and the need for systematic follow-up and long-term supports for many of the more chronically ill patients (Richmond, 1970). Later, study was made of the feasibility of direct placements into satellite housing of patients who were not graduates of the halfway house. Experience showed that many persons, who previously were thought to require the structure and supervision of the halfway house, functioned quite adequately in satellite housing. An increasing number of patients referred from hospitals and other psychiatric agencies were placed directly in small housing units, such as apartments, duplexes, and small homes scattered throughout the county, bypassing admission to the halfway house. The availability of both halfway house and satellite housing units enhances flexibility of placement choice. The existence of a large number of community apartments increases the possibility that roommates can be matched in terms of age, personality, and level of functioning. Three to six individuals of the same sex reside together, do their own shopping, cooking, and housework. Usually the housing units are found by the agency staff. The lease may be held by the residents, by the agency, or jointly, cosigned by both the residents and the agency. When residents hold the lease they pay rent directly to the landlord. Otherwise they often pay rent to the agency which in turn pays the landlord. Staff members specifically assigned to the Satellite Housing Program are available as needed for guidance and counseling of residents, both individually and in groups. Staff members are also available on a twenty-four-hour, on-call basis for emergency situations. Generally, the residents of three or four apartments comprise a stable group which meets with staff members a minimum of once every two weeks. Groups are hosted by the residents themselves on a rotating basis in their own housing units. Interim group meetings are often held by the members of a single housing unit without staff present. Satellite housing staff maintains liaison with therapists and agencies such as the day treatment center or sheltered workshop with which the residents are involved. Often early intervention, precipitated by a call of concern from a roommate, can prevent rehospitalization. Occasionally a resident in significant crisis may be removed from his apartment and placed for a brief period in El Camino House as an alternative to hospitalization.

The program provides both transitional and long-term housing and aftercare services. For some residents, the satellite housing units become their permanent homes, with varying amounts of ongoing supervision. Sometimes the agency is simply on call, the residents having, for all intents and purposes, reached independent living. Others leave the program to live entirely on their own.

Like El Camino House, the Satellite Housing Program is a high expectation setting. Residents in satellite housing units contract in writing with the agency to remain in outpatient therapy,

129

to attend the regularly scheduled meetings with other residents, and to occupy their time constructively. Of course, levels of expectation are always geared to the individual's level of functioning and his potential. For instance, even after long periods in a vocational rehabilitation program, some residents are unable to manage more than a half-time placement in a sheltered workshop. They, nevertheless, remain in the satellite housing program but with lower goals than those of less disabled residents. Sometimes they are transferred to other housing units to live with individuals with similar problems under close supervision from the visiting staff.

Many patients now placed in boarding and family care homes could be placed in satellite housing and at less cost to themselves and their financial sponsors. Group, family care, and boarding homes have been with us for centuries, along with the idea that live-in, twenty-four-hour staff supervision is a necessity. Some mental health professionals hesitate to refer their disturbed, dependent, and inadequate patients to a setting which seems to provide less supervision and counseling than traditional settings, despite the twenty-four-hour availability of staff. A major part of our work, then, is the continuing interpretation of such programs to referring agencies and professionals.

There are some patients who prefer or even insist upon discharge from the hospital to the community without any plan for appropriate housing. Often they live alone in a rooming house or transient hotel, or they return to a chaotic family situation. Many of these patients are quite fearful of and resist referral to a halfway house. However, when they are properly informed and oriented while still in the hospital, many find the idea of living fairly independently in a small satellite housing unit, with perhaps only two or three others, a quite attractive alternative to their previous plans. Thus, many patients who might otherwise be lost to sound aftercare planning can be brought into a posthospital rehabilitation program.

The use of small, semi-independent, supervised housing is an emerging development in the field of aftercare services. It provides a desirable alternative to the use of custodial boarding and family care homes. In some cases it also can be an alternative to hospitalization. In addition, finding apartments, duplexes, or cottages for small groups of patients is a simple task indeed when compared with the work involved in recruiting adequate family care and supervised boarding homes or in establishing halfway houses. Zoning problems and special licensing regulations are not involved, since the use made of satellite housing dwellings is not significantly different from the use that would be made of them by any other citizen.

The importance of having a range of facilities cannot be overemphasized. A combination of a halfway house and a satellite housing program gives the agency great flexibility and enables it to serve persons with many different needs for supervision and support. Another agency which illustrates this is Transitional Services, Inc., of Pittsburgh, Pennsylvania. This agency provides three types of residential services: two halfway houses; two supervised apartment buildings, each with full time resident staff; and twenty-seven independent apartments located throughout the community. The program expected to achieve total capacity of two hundred residents in the spring of 1971. "The types of facilities . . . are not established necessarily in a graduated sequence. Flexibility is maintained to allow for direct placement in any facility as well as movement from one to another according to individual needs and circumstances at any given time. No time limit is established for residents in any facility; however, an attitude of movement toward independent living is maintained with each resident" (Brochure of Transitional Services, Inc.).

The CORP research project (Community Oriented Remotivation Program) of the Fort Logan Community Mental Health Center in Denver is another example of the planned movement of groups of patients from the hospital to apartments in the community. Here, the scattered apartment concept is an integral part of a comprehensive social and vocational rehabilitation program. This three-phase program uses a halfway house on the grounds of the hospital as an intermediate step between inpatient status and supervised community living.

One of the central purposes of the program is to train the

patient to live in the community in a stable and independent way. The first, or Hospital and Teaching Phase, consists of forming "intentional family groups" of two to four hospitalized patients of the same sex, which then become involved in a highly structured teaching program on the essentials of community living. The second, or CORP Apartment Phase, involves moving these groups of patients to the halfway house on the grounds of the hospital. The building was remodeled into six self-contained apartments, thus simulating the conditions of community apartment living. During this phase there is a deemphasis on formal structured classes and an increase of intentional family group meetings and use of the hospital industrial therapy programs.

The third, or Community-Based Phase, involves transfer of the intentional family groups into apartments in the community. The patient in the community is closely followed by staff, usually through the medium of intentional family group counseling. More recently, groups assigned to the research program skipped the halfway house phase and moved directly from the hospital to the community phase (Liss, 1969). A major feature of the program is a "no discharge policy," based on the recognition that the chronically ill patient needs long-term help even after he is relocated in the community. Therefore CORP patients are not routinely discharged from aftercare services, except at their own insistence, no matter how adequate the patient's adjustment appears to be.

Looking Ahead

Goertzel (1965) states:

The need for halfway houses for returned patients increases as a result of the pressures upon mental hospital staffs to keep their populations down and the resultant failure to rehabilitate their patients sufficiently before returning them to the community. The need for posthospital services is further increased as society becomes more complex and the social, intellectual, and interpersonal skills required to participate in it increase concomitantly, resulting in more and more people being unable to participate without guidance, help, or support. Increased numbers of people can function only in a simplified milieu. The halfway house represents an attempt to keep the returned mental patient functioning with a minimum amount of further dislocation.

Although the need for halfway houses is vast, we may question whether halfway houses in their present form are not outmoded as aftercare facilities since they cannot even begin to meet the need. Each of the more than two hundred small, intimate houses accommodates between twelve and twenty residents at a time, or perhaps thirty-five to sixty persons over a year's period. No matter how attractive in style and noble in purpose, they cannot hope to serve more than a fraction of the total number of persons requiring service, and then, in their present form, they serve only one segment of that population; the single, divorced, or otherwise unattached person. It has been estimated that "if the time were to come when as many as 100,000 of the half million who are now inpatients were to be living in halfway houses, there would need to be about 5,000 [halfway houses]—more than twenty-five times the present number" (Glasscote, Gudeman, and Elpers, 1971). But halfway houses are difficult to establish, primarily because of problems of funding and zoning. Provision of funding to stimulate and facilitate the establishment of more halfway houses, if it is to have any real impact on the movement, would have to involve large amounts of money, probably from federal or state grants. Even if such funds were forthcoming, there is the danger of deterioration of the halfway house movement should it become involved in a rigid bureaucratic structure. The special character of halfway houses, their intimacy, enthusiasm, and innovativeness, might be lost. As Apte (1968) pointed out, the provision of such funds under the National Mental Health Act in England led to the proliferation of halfway houses which were, in time, largely unused, poorly staffed, nontransitional in nature, and lacking in dynamic treatment procedures.

Community attitudes toward the housing of deviant groups in the community, although changing, are not changing quickly enough. All houses encounter some level of opposition in the community to the existence of the house. More permissive zoning ordinances, although quite desirable, are not likely on a large scale, nor are they a guarantee of community acceptance.

The development of well planned scattered housing programs holds the potential for beginning to fill the gap in needed residential services. There is no inherent limitation, as there is in halfway houses, on the number of persons which can be accommodated at one time since, theoretically at least, the program can procure for lease as many additional apartments as necessary. The major limitation, as always, is lack of funds to provide adequate staffing. But with proper staff coverage, supervision too can be graded according to the needs of the individuals living in a housing unit, with some units presumably requiring more intensive and regular contact than others.

As stated earlier, no special zoning is required and satellite housing programs offer considerable advantage to the sponsoring organization as well as to the patient. The programs are relatively low in cost; even occupants on welfare, by sharing with roommates, are usually able to assume the full cost of rent, food, and utilities. Major expenditures in addition to staff salaries include funds to pay the rent when the units are not filled, rental deposits on newly procured housing, staff transportation expenses, and the cost of office space and equipment. However, since the housing units are developed gradually as the need arises, large initial outlays of funds for physical facilities are avoided.

Family groups too, either intact or single-parent, can be accommodated in scattered housing units, thus significantly broadening services to groups not characteristically accommodated in supervised residences.

Although traditional halfway houses still are needed to serve those patients who require, at least initially, the special familylike environment and proximity to staff characteristic of the halfway house, scattered or satellite housing often can substitute for the halfway house, and the development of such programs should help meet the urgent need for increased therapeutic housing. Halfway houses in combination with scattered supervised housing hold the promise of serving a larger number and a wider range of individuals and groups than hitherto served. Such a combination makes it possible to offer rehabilitation housing not on the basis of what is available but on the basis of patients' needs, goals, and level of functioning.

CHAPTER 7

Social Rehabilitation

H. Richard Lamb, Victor Goertzel

What is there to say about social rehabilitation? Who would argue against it? At first glance it is a noble concept. But discussions of it too often deteriorate into a series of fine sounding but basically empty generalities. Our goal in this chapter is to get at the essence of this elusive concept. Basically, social rehabilitation, or social therapy or social treatment as it is often called, is aimed at decreasing social isolation and improving the ability to interact with others. It may take many forms, ranging from group recreational activities to helping people learn or relearn such basic skills of community living as how to use public transportation, how to budget, and how to shop for food. When apathy, dependence, and withdrawal are the most prominent symptoms, social therapy may be the treatment of choice.

To what extent should we urge people to socialize, both in social treatment programs and in their lives outside of treatment?

This is not an easy question to answer. Certainly socialization makes life more meaningful than it may otherwise be. But many chronic patients left to their own devices, alone or with a tolerant host, often maintain an isolated existence. As noted in Chapter One, Freeman and Simmons (1963) contend that such tolerance not only fails to reduce bizarre behavior but may encourage it. We must recognize, however, that we cannot force people to socialize. If a person clearly and consistently lets us know that he does not want to improve his social skills and to spend time with other people, the choice is his. Under these circumstances, he should withdraw from the social therapy program until he decides that he wants to make use of it. The door to reentering the program should be left open; and his refusal to use this part of the program should not cause us to be less willing to offer him other services such as vocational programs and medication. Many people who do well in a vocational program are not able to, or choose not to, do well in the social sphere.

At the same time participation in a social therapy program on evenings and weekends should not be contingent upon participation in the vocational program of a rehabilitation center. If someone is not ready to participate in the vocational program or, indeed, chooses to opt out of the world of work altogether, he should still be welcome at social and recreation activities; such a person should simply be excluded from the rehabilitation center during weekdays set aside for work. The important thing is to offer to those who have few or no social skills or are too frightened to attempt to socialize or both an opportunity in a sheltered setting to develop the ability to relate to others.

In social treatment, change in behavior is generated by the relatively high and continually increasing demands made by the treatment program and its staff. Their expectations are that the patient will realize his potential for socialization, whatever that potential may be. This treatment can involve recognizing that the patient's potential is low and settling for this low level, but nothing less. A word of warning is needed here. A middle-class, intellectually oriented professional staff can all too easily interpret high expectations in terms of verbal sophistication and the ability to participate "meaningfully" in group therapy. Such an orientation excludes from the program many regressed, older, or nonverbal schizophrenics, persons for whom social rehabilitation is vital.

Most social rehabilitation programs are oriented toward discouraging isolation, passivity, morbid introspection, and preoccupation with the past. They generally include a social milieu, utilize at least some of the principles of the therapeutic community as discussed in Chapter One, and emphasize group activities designed to enhance interaction, restore responsibility, and encourage independence. They deal primarily with behavior not with intrapsychic change and can modify the symptoms that result from long periods in an impersonal total institution (Zusman, 1969); these symptoms of institutionalization include lack of initiative, apathy, withdrawal, oversubmissiveness to authority, excessive dependence upon the institution, and feelings of worthlessness and dehumanization.

In general, social treatment programs produce favorable results with chronic psychotic populations, particularly in improving social functioning and in increasing hospital release rates. A widely accepted rationale for social treatment is that socializing experiences can to some extent overcome the profound ego deficits of the schizophrenic. The lack of those intact portions of the personality which are needed to cope with the demands of the world may well leave the person disabled in the social sphere and sorely in need of establishing adaptive behavior patterns consistent with cultural norms. The apathy, dependence, and withdrawal characteristic of the chronic schizophrenic patient for the most part respond well to social therapy. Patients find they can talk to professionals when they are engaged in a common task, in particular a concrete task such as a manual activity or a game of checkers. Here, the direct focus is on the task rather than on the patient (Beard, Goertzel, and Pearce, 1958). This situation does not generate pressure to keep the conversation going continuously, as a strictly verbal psychotherapy situation does. Further, the patient may be more proficient at the task than the professional is; the patient then can be self-confident and can even assume a leadership role. There is also a parallel between social therapy and play therapy, where, for instance, the child can talk about how a doll feels rather than how he himself feels. Finally, social rehabilitation reaches large numbers of patients, an important factor in the treatment of the chronic mentally ill for whom trained staff is more often than not in short supply.

Growing evidence also indicates, however, that hospital-based social therapies do not increase the patient's chances of remaining in the community (Sanders, Smith, and Weinman, 1967; Fairweather, Sanders, Maynard, and Cressler, 1969; Fairweather, 1964). And although social rehabilitation in the hospital improves somewhat the community adjustment of long-term patients, these patients still show major inadequacies in functioning while in the community. Sanders, Smith, and Weinman (1967), in their post-hospital study of chronic patients, found that the majority were unemployed and that the few who had obtained full-time employment were able to earn only submarginal wages. Leisure activities reflected almost no involvement with others, interpersonal contacts were highly curtailed, and group affiliations were almost nonexistent. Thus, hospital-based social treatment is not sufficient to prevent rehospitalization or to enable long-term patients to make an adequate community adjustment. There is a clear need for community-based social treatment to sustain and further gains made in the hospital. Rehabilitation in the community overcomes a major shortcoming of rehabilitation in the hospital, namely that the patient becomes too dependent on and involved with the protected world of the hospital if he remains too long. The realities of the outside world seem all the more harsh by contrast; and the patient may beat a hasty retreat to the sanctuary of the hospital, rather than attempt to deal with the problems of adjustment to the community.

Let us look at such a patient returning to the community. He may be impoverished in his social life and experience difficulty in reestablishing satisfactory interpersonal relationships. The fact that the community provides a wide range of formal arrangements and facilities for social interaction is no guarantee that he will use them. For instance, his boarding home may be next door to a YMCA, but he may never enter the building, let alone use its facilities. A first step in his social rehabilitation may be to help him make contact with and use the community resources near him. However, if he is not ready for this step, then a program such as that provided by a day treatment center or expatient social club should be considered.

Such community-based rehabilitation programs provide a sheltered, relatively nonthreatening social environment. The group is composed primarily of individuals who share the experience of mental illness. This common denominator of previous psychiatric hospitalization may help in the formation of a high degree of group solidarity since people with similar experiences and problems tend to be mutually accepting and supportive of each other. Expectations of the members are not as high or as persistently maintained as they are in the community at large. Deviance, such as many of the overt manifestations of mental illness, is tolerated more readily than it is in the community (Goertzel, Beard, and Pilnick, 1960; Wechsler, 1961).

The words of an expatient vividly describe the situation (Bachmann, 1971):

During the reentry period, fellow expatients are the only people you know who are capable of understanding your moods, doubts, and fears, and whom you can rely on to be tolerant of your social shortcomings. But you have been assured that you must divorce yourself from them and make new friends *if you are to continue to progress. So you feel guilty about clinging to them, but how else are you to fill up this vacuum? Their solace, advice, companionship, encouragement, and evaluation are of great benefit to you. To be sure, you are subject to their precipitous ups and downs, as they are to yours. But even in their precarious situations they seem to be able to respond to your needs more easily than other people do.*

While the group is an essential part of social treatment, a perplexing problem for expatient social clubs and aftercare programs in particular is the composition of these groups. If all the patients appear very sick, other less chronic and less severely ill persons may hesitate to join; they may not want to identify themselves with such a group. Rightly or wrongly they may conclude that they have nothing in common. But these people also may not have the social capabilities to utilize regular community facilities.

This problem points up the need for professional leadership and volunteers to dilute what can otherwise be an oppressive atmosphere of chronicity. Those who run social rehabilitation programs should be concerned about the effects of labeling. When the participant is seen both by the community and by himself as still being in the patient role, his identity as a patient rather than as a "normal" member of the community is solidified. Several steps can be taken to minimize labeling. The staff and participants of social rehabilitation programs can emphasize that the program is a transitional one in which the expatient participates for a limited period until he is ready to go on to the social facilities in the community used by everyone. The social treatment program should also, if possible, be located in a community facility, such as a church or a YMCA. Even if there are no nonpatients there at the same time, the fact that the program is not located in a hospital or mental health center emphasizes the transitional nature of the program and the fact that it is not so different from the regular social activities of the community. If these measures to minimize labeling are diligently employed, social rehabilitation programs do not usually segregate patients from the nonpatient community and keep expatients from using community facilities.

Wolkon (1970), however, found that the typical client of a rehabilitation center is a chronically dependent person. And it is our experience that these programs attract persons who will not or cannot use community facilities, persons who would otherwise segregate themselves in a hotel room or boarding home or their own back bedroom. For many severely psychiatrically handicapped persons, participating in a social therapy program may be the extent of their social capabilities (Lamb and Goertzel, 1971). These observations bring into focus an important question: Are rehabilitation programs in the community truly focusing on rehabilitation, or are they simply segregated maintenance programs for stabilized chronically dependent and regressed persons? For a graphic example of this problem and how it can be resolved, see the section on Horizon House later in this chapter. In brief, it is crucial to maintain expectations that the client will realize his potential and will move as soon as he is able beyond the rehabilitation center. As noted in Chapter One in the discussion of minimizing the labeling process, it must be made clear to him that he is not just a mental patient, but a person with strengths which will allow him to take his place in society.

If used effectively, volunteers can be extremely helpful in facilitating this transition of the expatient to regular community life. Volunteers freely mingle and interact with members and take part in group activities. The expatient thus gains experience in relating to "normal" nonprofessional members of the community. In some cases volunteers function as leaders or coleaders of specific groups, primarily those where they have interest or skills to contribute. Equally important is the element of community involvement that they give to the agency (Glasscote, Cumming, and others, 1971). The presence of volunteers demonstrates to members that the community is interested in expatients as people, an interest that paid staff often cannot fully convey. A particularly innovative way of using volunteers, the Thresholds social placement program, is described later in this chapter.

However, volunteers are often persons seeking help for themselves but unable to acknowledge or accept their need for help. If the club leaders are aware of this phenomenon, they can use it to good advantage. For instance, Joshua Bierer (1948), the British psychiatrist who pioneered in therapeutic social clubs, describes inviting friends and relatives of patients to become members of an expatient social club so that the membership would not consist entirely of ex-mental hospital patients. Many of these relatives and friends became, for all intents and purposes, patients. The club thus performed a service to these persons, who, while not identified as patients with overt symptoms and manifestations of illness, were obviously in need of social therapy.

142

Social Rehabilitation

A controversial issue involved here is whether expatient clubs and aftercare programs should be led by patients or staff. Those who argue for patient-led programs point out that many expatients are capable of running their own groups and that giving expatients leadership roles promotes initiative and responsibility. The expatient acquires experience which stands him in good stead as he makes the transition to independence in the community. He also derives much satisfaction from and takes considerable pride in his club's being independent. Patient-led clubs, since they do not require scarce, expensive professional time, are economical to operate. Professionally led programs generally cannot be self-supporting and therefore require outside subsidy.

Where the program is staff led, the professionals or volunteers or both screen prospective members to determine whether social therapy is appropriate for them and whether they are ready for the particular program. The staff uses its expertise and its knowledge of each member to ensure that he is participating in those parts of the program that are most helpful to him. Where the member needs services in addition to social therapy, such as medication, individual or group psychotherapy, vocational programs, and transitional housing, the staff tells him where and how to apply for them. In some instances, professionals running social therapy programs provide these services themselves. Staff serves also to control disruptive behavior. For instance, aggressive, paranoid persons may gain control of an expatient club and use it to serve their own power needs without regard for the therapeutic needs of the other members. The other members may find that they no longer have a voice in running the club and that they are being used to undermine the influence of staff or other natural patient leaders. Such a situation tends to drive the passive schizophrenic patient from the club, thus depriving him of a therapeutic resource which he sorely needs. In such circumstances, if staff is in a position of responsibility in the club, it may interpret this situation to the total membership. If the members are still unable to oppose the aggressive paranoid members, then the staff may use its authority to deal with the disruptive members.

Rehabilitation in Community Mental Health

Our own view is that programs should be staff led with ex-patients being given as much responsibility as they can handle. The more chronic the group of expatients, the more staff leadership is necessary. To have effective patient leadership at all, one must avoid a homogeneous group of chronic patients and have a mixed group that includes persons who are less chronic, passive, and dependent. In general, we feel that the members should be involved in planning for short-term projects such as the weekly programs and activities but that formulating the long-term goals of the agency, such as rehabilitation rather than maintenance and emphasis on the transitional nature of the program, should be the responsibility primarily of staff. Indeed, if a patient is ready to lead in formulating long-term goals of high expectations and independence, is he not then ready to leave the ex-mental patient role and take his place in society in less sheltered and segregated settings?

So much for some of the general principles and problems of social rehabilitation programs in the community. The three examples of well developed programs below illustrate the varied forms which social therapy can take.

Horizon House in Philadelphia has an impressive, multi-faceted social and vocational rehabilitation program. Three aspects are especially noteworthy. The staff has an admirable ability to be honest about problems and shortcomings in their program and to take positive steps to correct them. They have developed a didactic program in the basic skills of community living which fills a vital need, especially for long-term psychiatric patients. They have the ability to combine high expectations with flexibility so that the agency can serve a full range of clients—the chronic, regressed, nonverbal schizophrenic as well as the young, verbal, "interesting" patient. In 1968, the staff began a series of self-evaluation investigations to assess the effectiveness of its programs. They came to the following conclusions (Rutman, 1970):

The total climate of the agency, though friendly, supportive, and comfortable, lacked a quality of vigor and purposefulness. The agency seemed on its way to becoming a haven in the community at which emotionally troubled persons could spend months or years in an unthreatening environment. There seemed little sense of movement through the program, little awareness of the importance of graduating. Our comfortable milieu—that aspect of our program that we had so highly valued—seemed, if anything, too soft and encompassing—and, inadvertently, dependency producing. We recognized that we were accepting—and in some cases catering to— a lack of commitment or motivation on the part of our clientele concerning their use of the program. Operating without criteria that could be applied to accepting, placing within, or graduating an individual from our agency, we had permitted a laissez faire climate to develop. This, we were concerned, served to perpetuate the individual's identification of himself as a psychiatric patient and impeded his relearning and development of a more positive self-regard.

The result was the development of a new philosophy and program. Thus, Horizon House now deems each client as being capable of making decisions that will affect his future progress and as an active and willing participant in the agency program. They expect the client to be motivated to complete the program and to make a commitment of time, effort, and money (on a sliding-scale basis). One year is the maximum time for a client's rehabilitation program, though in practice clients have not been held rigidly to this time limit if they are making good use of the program. The new philosophy assumes that every client admitted to Horizon House is a likely candidate for personal, social, and vocational rehabilitation, regardless of the degree of chronicity and regression at the outset. Thus, all clients are expected to participate in all facets of the agency program, both social and vocational. The message is now given to clients that availing themselves of the program's activities is a privilege as much as a right and is contingent upon an individual's active involvement in his particular program.

Horizon House describes its new program as operating on an educational behavior-modification model. Their goal is to create a climate more akin to a community college than to an outpatient clinic, day hospital, or social agency. They want each client to view his rehabilitation experience as an opportunity to participate in a series of educational programs. Each client has a significant voice in selecting or deciding upon these activities, is expected to be present and on time, and must perform satisfactorily so that he graduates to the next higher level.

Experience has shown that clients do better and are more likely to stay with the program when they have staff with whom they can relate throughout their rehabilitation experience than when they do not. Thus, incoming clients are assigned to a team for the full program. Staff for the team consists of a vocational rehabilitation counselor, a social worker who sees each client individually depending on need, and a group counselor. The latter has groups consisting of people on all teams, and all group counselors meet once weekly so that information about how clients are progressing in all the groups can be fed back to each team staff. Group counselors are college graduates with interest and experience in groups; they generally do not have master's degrees. Each team, including both patients and staff, meets together for one and a half hours twice a week.

The program is a three-phase one; our interest in this chapter lies in the first two phases. A client may enter the program at any phase, depending on his needs. Phase 1 emphasizes basic remedial training in the fundamentals of everyday living and is intended for the most seriously regressed or chronic patients. This phase continues for three months, during which the client learns about home management, personal hygiene, and community resources. The sessions are informal with time allowed for discussion and putting newly learned skills into practice.

This educational program begins with the very basics of living. In the section on transportation, the client learns how to locate a street address, how houses are numbered, and how streets are arranged. The instruction details how to use public transportation—where the buses, subways, and trolleys run; where to get on; where to get off; how much the fare is; how to transfer from one bus to another; how to ask for directions; and how to use a map of the

146

city. Much of the instruction takes place on the streets of the city. The section on community resources includes such basic skills as using the telephone, how to apply for various social welfare benefits, and how to obtain community legal and medical services. Clients are taught how to shop, what to look for in stores, as well as how to avail themselves of the various kinds of entertainment in the community.

During Phase 1, the client additionally participates in a sheltered work program for ten hours per week. Also, the client, if ready, is assigned to his team group counseling sessions that meet one and a half hours twice per week. Others receive individual counseling until judged ready to participate in group counseling. Rehabilitation counseling also begins in Phase 1. Thus, this first phase involves the client in vocational orientation, training in basic interpersonal skills, classroom training in basic areas of community functioning, and a group counseling relationship that continues throughout his stay at Horizon House. All these activities require a maximum of twenty-five hours a week of the client's time.

In Phase 2, instruction in home management, personal hygiene, and community resources is continued, but the number of class hours is reduced substantially. Structured group sessions deal with such subjects as appropriate social behavior, problems in independent living, and relationships with the opposite sex, which include attempts to dispel misconceptions about sex, both delusional and naïve. A half-time sheltered job-training workshop experience is included. The Horizon House building was specifically designed for social and vocational rehabilitation. Within the building is a wide range of sheltered vocational activities. The facilities of the center itself are used as work placements including food service in the cafeteria and cleaning and maintenance of the building. In a well equipped rehabilitation workshop in the basement members work on a variety of subcontracts. In an area adjacent to the workshop members learn clerical skills, typing, use of office machines, and filing. The team group counseling program continues. Phase 3 involves the client almost full time in a vocational program in addition to his continuing group counseling program.

147

Rehabilitation in Community Mental Health

Horizon House expects each client to try to live up to his or her potential. But the staff also sees the need for flexibility. Although the emphasis is on groups, clients are worked with individually if the situation demands it. Further, the instruction dealing with such subjects as appropriate social behavior and relationships with the opposite sex is given in several sections, each designed for clients with different characteristics and needs. The staff in one section takes a concrete, highly structured approach suited for long-term, regressed, and very "brittle" clients. Another section covering the same subjects may delve more deeply into underlying problems and feelings. Only clients able to handle sophisticated attempts at self-awareness are included in the latter sessions. Moreover, if a client is not ready or not motivated for any group stressing self-awareness and social skills, he need not participate as long as he remains committed to the total program including the vocational parts. The goal of Horizon House is to enrich the client's entire life, both social and vocational, but clients are not driven away if they are not yet ready for working toward such sweeping goals. Perhaps of greatest importance is that by maintaining high expectations with flexibility, Horizon House does not exclude the long-term, nonverbal, unsophisticated client.

The ability to take a searching look at themselves has enabled the staff of this agency to develop a program that is comprehensive, meeting both social and vocational needs, and flexible, offering services to the chronic and acute, regressed and relatively intact. The program has progressed from simple maintenance of long-term psychiatric patients in a segregated setting to effective rehabilitation.

The second example, Thresholds in Chicago, began simply as a place in which withdrawn expatients could enjoy social relationships with each other; it evolved into a high expectations setting. Now its combined social and vocational rehabilitation program is time limited and thus transitional in nature. Members can remain in the program for a maximum of one year. They are then expected to be able to utilize community facilities. The time limit is flexible however. If a member has been in the program for a year

148

but is still making good use of it, he may be given an extension to continue working toward his particular rehabilitation goals. This is a comprehensive, multifaceted program. Here we focus on the unique social placement part of it. But first let us look at some of the important lessons learned by Thresholds as the program evolved.

Initially, Thresholds had minimal professional direction. Centered around the use of a lounge, activities were available to members on an as-you-wish basis and included cards, Scrabble, conversation, piano-playing, reading, pool, Ping-Pong, and listening to records. Coffee and refreshments were provided, and members could help themselves throughout the afternoon or evening. Supper, prepared by the members, was available at a nominal charge before the evening program twice a week and during the Sunday program. Volunteers were active in the lounge program, trying to relate to members over bridge and other games or engaging them in conversation.

Thresholds' description of its original lounge program (Dincin and Swift, 1967) illustrates some of the techniques often used in social therapy:

The lounge meets the needs of members at a number of levels along the continuum of increasing ability to participate in social relationships. For the new member who needs an opportunity to observe without active participation, the lounge provides the quiet corner necessary for this observation. A magazine can protect the member from intrusion by others. For the member a little more comfortable with others, a game of Scrabble can be a more or less socially demanding activity, depending on the individual's own wish. The volunteer participating in the activity will be sensitive to the member's wish (or need) to limit his participation to taking his turn or to join in a more general conversation between plays. Conversation carried on over coffee may be superficial, related to such general topics as the weather or the problems of public transportation, or it may involve an important sharing of personal interests between two members. Staff and volunteers work to provide the opportunity for relationships that the member needs at the moment. If the members

149

can seek this out and provide it for one another, this is all to the good and is the eventual goal of the program. If they cannot, staff or volunteers step in.

While the lounge program provided a variety of levels of socialization, it was also relatively unstructured. Many long-term psychiatric persons, with disorganized thought processes, need a structured program. For some the lounge program was confusing and even overwhelming in the number of choices offered. Further, there was little movement, and expatients tended to remain in the program for years; passivity and dependence rather than rehabilitation were being fostered. The mere existence of a lounge in which expatients are present does not constitute a social rehabilitation program. Members can hide in the lounge, remain isolated and withdrawn from meaningful social relationships. Thus this program was discontinued.

A definite allocation of staff and volunteer time is required to make a center into an arena for the development of appropriate social behavior; a new structured activity program at Thresholds has proven to be an effective aid in this direction. Activities include the Thresholds newspaper, arts and crafts, cooking and baking, social and folk dancing. An activity such as elementary cooking may help members learn the basic skills of living in the community. The group can plan the menu, draw up a budget, do the shopping, and then prepare the meal. In other instances, such as copper-enameling or working on the newspaper, the particular activity serves as a focus of attention, and the individual can relate to the activity itself rather than to other individuals if this is his need. It also provides a topic of conversation, a role to play, and motions to go through. The leader structures the situation for the member by providing goals, by sometimes directing the activity, and, when necessary, by setting limits.

Groups are centered around an activity the members can enjoy, as well as being designed to fill their specific basic needs. Thresholds groups allow members to be active or passive participants in various activities. They can join large groups or small

150

groups, depending on their readiness to be involved in social relationships of different complexities. Some of the groups require a great deal of personal participation by members, while others allow them to maintain a relative distance. Some groups involve members in manual and physical activities; others are based on verbal communication; and still others allow the members to communicate through writing. Most of the groups are for both men and women, although a few are primarily for members of one sex. Some groups encourage members to participate in activities outside the building, in some cases in a very carefully planned, structured way, and in other cases, in a very casual, independent manner.

The main thrust at Thresholds is in the high expectations social and vocational rehabilitation program. But there is also recognition of the need to provide services to those not motivated to participate in a high expectations program and a recognition of the fact that more persons require help than the forty to forty-five clients the staff can serve at one time in their intensive program. Thus, this agency has set up a satellite center, run by a small and largely nonprofessional staff, in a neighborhood where thousands of ex-state hospital patients live impoverished lives in large residential hotels and boarding homes. At this satellite center, expectations are lower, the program is less transitional and less intensive. Many persons, however, have been given an opportunity to enrich their lives in a social activity program; many have been motivated to participate in sheltered vocational programs.

Many members attend and do well in the social rehabilitation program within the protected setting of the agency. But they are fearful about moving out into the normal social activities of the community. When they try they are frequently unsuccessful or prefer the familiar and sheltered activities of Thresholds. The social placement program was begun to bridge this gap. In this program, volunteers from the community are matched by Thresholds staff with individual members on a one-to-one basis. The volunteer and the member then go into the community together to such places as bowling alleys, nonpatient social organizations, museums, and parks. The volunteer has the Thresholds staff available to discuss the goals

151

of the activity, how to work with the member, and any problems that might arise. An attempt is made by staff to match volunteers and members who are compatible and where there is felt to be the best chance for a therapeutic result. Hopefully, the member will be able, eventually, to continue the same activities, on his own, without the volunteer.

The volunteer is not given any extensive information about the member's psychiatric history but is told about his interests and given suggestions as to activities that might serve to start a relationship. They meet for the first time in the agency, usually introduced to each other by a staff member. This meeting is relatively informal one, frequently over a cup of coffee; it is designed to put both client and volunteer at ease. The volunteers are requested to devote one evening weekly to the activity. Even though the ultimate goal is to join together in an ongoing community organization, a relationship must first develop between the two individuals. Therefore, it is not unusual for them to meet for several weeks casually over coffee, for dinner, or to go to a concert, a movie, or some free activity in the area. The volunteer and member go as friends. Therefore, each one pays his own way. Volunteers are not permitted to consistently pay for or give things to members since this is not the way normal relationships develop within the community. Volunteers commit themselves to six months with a member, although in some cases much more or less time is needed. Members and volunteers are encouraged to call each other and to relate to each other as any two friends would.

After the initial phase of getting to know each other, the activity is not going to a one-shot event, such as a ball game or a dance, but participating in an ongoing social organization that meets regularly. They may join a church group, a bowling league, a special interest club, a class, a hobby group, or another regularly scheduled activity. And they go, not as expatient and volunteer, but as two friends. In this way the member can begin to face a new social situation because of the support from a socially adept person with whom he has already developed a relationship.

Our final example is the Philadelphia Enabler Program,

based at the Philadelphia State Hospital. It grew out of a controlled comparative study of three hospital treatment programs together with a three-year follow-up study of the patients who had experienced these programs (Sanders, Smith, and Weinman, 1967). Conclusions about the effectiveness of structured socioenvironmental treatment led to the application of these concepts in a social treatment program in the community. This program centers about extensive use of indigenous community members given special training to be enablers (Weinman, Sanders, Kleiner, and Wilson, 1970) and focuses on long-term functional psychotic patients with characteristic symptoms of apathy, isolation, and dependency. Long-term patients are defined as persons who have had at least two years of accumulated hospitalization. The average length of hospitalization of the patients who participate is twelve years, and the average education is through the eighth grade. Each patient receives twelve weeks of orientation while still in the hospital on a special rehabilitation unit to prepare him for community living. This orientation deals wth such matters as personal grooming, basic cooking, budgeting, and community resources. Each patient is assigned a therapist who sees him both in group and individual counseling during this period and is responsible for placing the patient in the community with an enabler appropriate for the case. Most enablers are middle-aged housewives, indigenous to the neighborhood in which the long-term patient is placed. Their children have grown, and these women are seeking not only a source of income but also an activity that will add meaning to their lives. A few enablers are young, non-professionally trained persons who want to develop careers in the mental health field. Prior to being assigned patients, enablers receive a five-week orientation course, and afterward they maintain contact with professionals. The enablers learn to structure the patient's home environment so that it is conducive to social interaction, to provide training in the specific skills necessary for survival in the community—how to shop, how to manage money, how to use banking facilities, and how to deal with landlords—and to coordinate the activities of patients so that they make use of community resources and service agencies.

153

Rehabilitation in Community Mental Health

There are two kinds of enablers, visiting and live in. Where visiting enablers are used, the patients are placed in apartments in groups of two or three and are visited by an enabler two hours daily five days a week. Visiting enablers are paid. Each group of patients has the services of a visiting enabler for one year only. Live-in enablers have patients living in their homes. They are reimbursed by the patients through welfare or other funds. Although the live-in enabler is comparable in many ways to the operator of boarding and family-care homes, the crucial difference is in orientation, training, and supervision. They see their function not simply as custodial care but as enabling the long-term patient's social integration into the normal community. How do the two enabler programs compare in regard to outcome? Preliminary indications are that they are comparable in effectiveness in reducing hospital readmission rates. Both programs enhance self-esteem more than hospital treatment does. Not surprisingly, the visiting enabler situation is more effective than is the live-in situation in generating independent behavior.

Both kinds of enablers, however, exert considerable influence in modifying the social behavior of the long-term patient. Because they generally share with the patient common socioeconomic and educational backgrounds, they can, in many respects, more easily communicate with the patient than can professionals. They can spend large periods of time supervising the patient's daily activities, thus helping to overcome the problem posed by the shortage of professional staff to provide community treatment.

The enabler program has achieved considerable success in helping long-term patients manage the daily problems of living, in mobilizing them to utilize community resources, and in preventing their return to the hospital. This is an impressive program. Our major reservation is that initially there is little emphasis on vocational rehabilitation. The staff of this program, however, feels that becoming weaned from the hospital and institutionalization and becoming integrated into the community are as much as these long-term, severely ill patients can handle at the beginning. At the end of eight months of treatment in the community program, patients who are judged employable either are referred to vocational rehabilitation or are assisted in finding employment. This judgment is made by the staff members who supervise the enablers. To date (personal communication, 1971) 19 per cent of patients at the point of completion of the one-year community treatment are in paid employment, about half full time and half part time. This is a significant result for this population of long-term patients.

We have discussed several sophisticated, comprehensive social therapy programs, but social therapy may also be effective on a much smaller and simpler scale as part of an aftercare program in a community mental health center or as a club for patients leading isolated lives in boarding homes. In some instances, a social worker may, with the help of volunteers from the local mental health association, organize a social club for his own clients. The club may meet in a church, YMCA, or boarding homes on a rotating basis. In fact, the well established organizations described in this chapter had simple beginnings. Another example, Fountain House, evolved from a volunteer-assisted club formed by expatients from one state hospital who met on the steps of the public library into its present comprehensive rehabilitation program with a million dollar building. Whether one has a million dollar building or simply has access to a church basement, social rehabilitation is a crucial part of the whole process of rehabilitation.

CHAPTER **8**

Evaluation of Rehabilitation Programs

Victor Goertzel

❧❧❧❧❧❧❧❧❧❧❧❧❧❧❧❧❧❧❧

$\mathbf{N}$ew programs in health, education, and welfare are being started throughout the country. The growing acceptance of social responsibility has generated an unprecedented mass of legislation dealing with man's welfare. Much of it was overdue and allows for services critically needed. On the other hand, a considerable amount of it does not live up to its claims and, in reality, is neither new nor of any real value. There must be constant examination of rehabilitation programs in order to assure their continuing value, and to determine when changes need to be made. This chapter deals with the necessity for evaluation research and the problems that arise in carrying it out and utilizing it in a meaningful way.

156

Evaluation of Rehabilitation Programs

Most research and demonstration efforts in health and welfare supported by public funds include a requirement that their worth be assessed. In reality, agencies and government often overlook evaluation in their eagerness to implement new programs intuitively believed to be worthwhile. When the evaluation requirement is not met, however, it is never known to what extent, if any, the services are effective and large sums of money are spent on programs without producing any useful knowledge about what works or what does not work. We must prevent haphazard programming by planning evaluation so that each project we undertake adds to our body of knowledge about services to people.

Objective evaluation is necessary because without it we become dependent upon our subjective impressions and are influenced by our biases. We remember the things that fit in with our preconceptions and forget those which are in conflict with our beliefs. In addition, most rehabilitation workers feel that their work is important and has a positive influence on their clients. One of the purposes of scientific research methods is to minimize such subjective bias so that conclusions can be based on hard data. We know that every mental health professional, whatever his theoretical orientation and therapeutic methods, has some clients who improve and some who do not; no therapist is successful with all his patients. Therapists employ various treatment methods depending upon the needs of different patients, but depending also upon his own preferences, orientation, and needs. Objective evaluation determines which methods are helpful for which therapists and with which clients, as well as determining if the therapy itself has resulted in improvement.

A number of aspects of dealing with the administration of an agency are critical from the point of view of program evaluation. First, in order for program evaluation to be conducted in the agency there must be administrative support at all levels and willingness to undergo some inconvenience to facilitate the study. This seemingly obvious statement cannot be overemphasized; without firm and consistent administrative support, meaningful program evaluation cannot be done.

Rehabilitation centers and community mental health clinics

157

typically collect such data as the number of patients treated, how long they stayed in treatment, or turnover rates. They may include a rating of improvement at termination as compared with status at intake. These ratings are often done perfunctorily and inconsistently by clinicians using poorly defined, subjective criteria. Such statistics are easy to collect and actually tell more about efficiency of operation than they do about effectiveness of treatment. The computerization of clinical records will make it even easier to gather such statistics than it is at present. Genuine evaluative research involves more than simply counting noses. It must develop some objective criteria for assessing patients' functioning outside of the treatment setting, and after treatment has stopped, and for assessing the effects of services upon those who received them.

Controlled Studies

An agency that seriously wants to evaluate its effectiveness must engage in controlled studies and run the risk of finding that its total program, or some valued aspects of it, does not contribute to reaching stated objectives. This risk is particularly threatening to a prestigious agency which is generally satisfied with itself, with its reputation, and with its growth in terms of an increasing budget and number of clients served. One might ask why such an agency would be motivated to evaluate its program if it is so satisfied with itself. In an ideal world the answer would be: a universal craving for truth and knowledge. Unhappily, this craving is too often lacking. In most instances I feel such an agency undertakes an evaluation because it is certain that research will completely reinforce its conviction that its programs are superior and will thus supply objective proof to the world of its superiority. Another factor that leads agencies into research efforts is that having a research program adds to prestige and not having one leaves the agency open to criticism and suspicion.

A controlled study is one in which a number of persons are not exposed to the program, or to that part of the program being evaluated, but are exposed to as many as possible of the other conditions in the study. These persons constitute the control group, as opposed to the experimental group which is exposed to the program being studied. The purpose is to ensure that the effects under examination are not the results of differences in the persons served or of experiences other than the one in question. Thus the control group should be comparable to the experimental group in all respects except that it is not exposed to the program being studied. Rigorously controlled studies, of course, can be conducted only in the laboratory, but they can be approximated in real life. It is possible to conduct a controlled evaluation by establishing a control group among the applicants who are denied service by the agency. In all other respects they should be comparable to applicants accepted for service. This can be done by matching applicants on known significant variables, and assigning one member of each matched pair to the experimental (demonstration) group and one to the control (comparison) group.

Unhappily, there is no general agreement on which variables are significant in mental health and rehabilitation research. Initially comparable groups can still be obtained, however, without identifying the important variables, by using some method of random assignment. Those applicants who meet the clearly defined requirements for eligibility for service can be assigned to the research groups by the use of a table of random numbers or strictly by rotation. If subjects are assigned to the experimental and control groups on a straight rotation basis—that is, if every second referral falls into the experimental group—the treatment staff can easily know which assignment is next and may manipulate the sequence of referrals to get patients assigned to the program which the staff prefers for a particular patient. Random assignment is preferable; if any system other than true randomization is used, clinicians may attempt to beat the system to get patients into the treatment they subjectively "know" is best for them. Pre- and post-measures should be obtained on all subjects in the study, including the controls. Statistical tests should be made to determine that the groups do not differ with respect to demographic factors (age, sex, education, race, social class) or to important psychiatric and vocational history factors.

Mental health professionals show great resistance to denying service to eligible applicants. They subjectively know their services are necessary, despite the lack of objective validation. They also fear alienating referral sources by denying service for the purpose of research. However, when there are more applicants than can be handled, service must be denied even if no research is being done. Often the subterfuge of a waiting list is used to screen out applicants. With careful planning and dissemination of information, such a situation can be used to establish control groups for research purposes. Experience at Fountain House (Beard, et al., 1963) shows that "controlled research can be done in voluntary service organizations without alienating either clientele or referral sources." As a matter of fact, most referral sources prefer a straight answer of accepted now or not accepted to the run-around of the waiting list!

It is usually not necessary to create a no-treatment control group. The control group can receive the usual or established treatment with the experimental group receiving a different kind of treatment. The comparison can then be made between the new method and the established method. For example, if a vocational counseling service is about to open a sheltered workshop, the contribution of the workshop to the employability of clients can be evaluated by randomly assigning some of the counselees who are felt to need a workshop experience to the service and evaluating its effect on them by comparing them with the clients who are not assigned to the workshop but who receive the other services of the agency. In practice, this is rarely, if ever, done. The counseling service believes it knows which clients need workshop experience and assigns these clients to the new facility. The counselors resist sending only a portion of the clients they "know" need this service or sending any persons they "know" do not need it. Thus, the value of the workshop as an added service cannot be determined. The agency has become impervious to objective data. It has no way of knowing whether or not the particular workshop is effective or whether or not the right clients are being referred to it.

Evaluation of Rehabilitation Programs

After the study is designed and goes into operation, the researcher must be constantly on guard to oppose programs and procedures that could render the evaluation useless. As I have noted, mental health professionals sincerely believe that they know which treatment is most effective for which patient. Anyone who has conducted a controlled study can cite dramatic instances of the pressures and tactics used to get favored subjects into programs contrary to the research plan. For instance, a social psychologist at an eastern university was called in as a research consultant on an ongoing study in a state prison. The prison researcher reported that because of administrative and clinical pressures a number of assignments to treatment groups were made contrary to the research design and asked, "What shall I do?" "Begin over again," was the reply. Making adjustments contrary to the research design renders the study invalid. Meaningful outcome evaluations can be achieved only if the researcher is aware of the many pitfalls and continually polices the study.

Making Research Meaningful

Genuine evaluative research, if it merely justifies existing programs, has not done enough. Even if it determines the effectiveness with which a program serves its particular clients, it has not done enough. Effort must be directed toward objectively examining the efficacy of the program. We must examine not only how well clients are served who come to us but also how great a contribution our program makes to solving a particular social problem, to meeting a particular need. For example, one social problem is the need for jobs for mental hospital patients returning to the community. A vocational rehabilitation program may serve two such persons a month out of the twenty who return to the community. If on the average one of these clients per month is placed in a job, the agency shows a superficially impressive fifty per cent success rate, but it is actually making only a five per cent (one in twenty) contribution to meeting the employment needs of all the mental hospital patients who return to the community during this period.

161

Rehabilitation in Community Mental Health

When an agency feels pressure to show "success," admission practices may be modified to select those of the target population most likely to succeed. This practice is known as "creaming." In extreme cases, the agency may select clients who would be successful without help—that is, those who would find and maintain employment without vocational rehabilitation services. Such a practice obviously excludes those, such as long-term ex-mental hospital patients, for whom full-time competitive employment is not immediately a realistic goal.

Similarly, in most state mental hospitals when innovative programs are introduced the patients selected are those having the best prognosis. Then the findings, based on work with the cream of the hospital population, are generalized, and the false conclusion is drawn that these new approaches work with the entire hospital population.

Community agencies and institutions also must be aware of whom they are including or excluding from service. The funding agencies should require rehabilitation facilities to report on the psychiatric, educational, economic, and other characteristics of the people who apply to, complete, and benefit from their programs. A case can be made for creaming insofar as only a portion of the needy population can be served. Nevertheless, a clear statement should be made of what specific population is being served, and some attempt should be made to describe the characteristics of that portion of the needy population not being served.

The false conclusion that can be drawn when creaming is practiced can be compounded by inadequate follow-up. For example, the state departments of rehabilitation justify their programs and budget in terms of numbers of clients placed on jobs. Their tendency is to close a case shortly after a client is employed without waiting to see if he is stabilized on the job. Some clients have no problem in getting jobs but are unable to keep them. Others, seeking to move up in the world of work, were employed at intake as well as at closing. To judge the success of a vocational rehabilitation program solely in terms of clients employed at closing is not sufficient.

Evaluation of Rehabilitation Programs

Program evaluation can focus on quality, process, or outcome. Each kind of evaluation has its own aims, strategies, and appropriate procedures; each results in different kinds of information; and each has its limitations and its usefulness. Quality evaluation studies of mental health programs are rare, probably because of difficulties in setting standards and measuring variables. By quality is meant the degree to which a treatment approaches some ideal standard. Process evaluation is conducted more commonly than quality evaluation. As its name suggests, it means evaluating the process by which the patient is treated and involves measurement of how well and how appropriately the accepted methods of treatment are applied. It should include such things as length of time between initial application for service and actual inception of service; length of time between request for vocational testing and actual administration of the tests, and between that and receipt of the test report; the variety of work situations to which the client is exposed during his workshop experience and the extent to which these follow a pattern of increasing complexity. Process evaluation is based upon an examination of agency case records. Unfortunately, the process may be good and the outcome poor. Or the records may be poor and yet the care provided is very good. Process evaluation, because it uses the accepted treatment methods as the standard or guide, tends to favor those who use conventional approaches and to penalize those who innovate and in their innovations deviate from the expected sequence of doing things.

Outcome evaluation is also complex. Many factors other than treatment influence outcome. However, as has been discussed in detail earlier in this chapter, we can be most certain of our evaluation if we have compared a group receiving a service with a comparable group which has not.

Hospital return rates were once regarded as really hard data, a clear index of treatment success or failure. A closer look, however, shows that return rates may be an incomplete measure of outcome. For example, expatients who felt that the original hospital treatment was ineffective may avoid going back to the hospital again or may seek alternative resources. Return to hospital may be more

163

closely related to the unwillingness of the family to put up with a troublesome family member than to the functioning level of the expatient. Or rehospitalization may be a temporary and therapeutic interlude in an ultimately successful rehabilitation program. Thus, what at first glance looks like a simple and important piece of hard data is not at all simple to interpret.

Similarly, employment presents problems as a major criterion for the success of vocational rehabilitation programs or of poverty programs. Employment rates can reflect a number of variables in addition to the particular program being evaluated. Obviously, availability of jobs is one factor. Another factor is age. It is well known how difficult it is to place many sixteen- to twenty-one-year-olds, but as they approach their middle twenties, they begin to disappear from the unemployment rolls and enter the job market. If evaluation of this particular age group is based upon comparisons of its employment history before and after exposure to a program, or to a series of programs over a fairly long time period, the observed success may be more apparent than real. Once again, the use of comparison groups of persons not receiving the service, in a controlled study, is the best means of determining the efficacy of a given treatment program. I reemphasize the importance of control groups made up of persons initially comparable on the significant variables and over the same time period.

Exposure to multiple programs is another complication in outcome evaluation. When many resources are available for a particular target population, whether it be disadvantaged youth or long-term mental hospital patients reentering the community, there is an inclination to shower programs upon the subjects. For example, a number of disadvantaged youths might be given a variety of programs with the goal of getting them into paying jobs. These programs could include class training to prepare for taking high school equivalency tests, prevocational work experience, a sports and outing program, a nutritional program including the serving of balanced hot lunches, and a summer camp experience. Even if the desired change occurs and is measured, it is almost impossible to sort out the relative contributions of the different programs to the outcome. This is an important issue if we want to learn the most efficient allocation of limited resources.

For purposes of research, resources may be available to provide this wealth of programs for a target group. However, when it comes to providing services to the whole population from which the sample is drawn, resources may be limited. Therefore, in research and demonstration projects the contribution of each separate program element must be determined and only those elements which contribute to the desired outcome developed for extended use. Required is a research design in which eligible clients are randomly assigned to one of several programs, specified combinations of programs, and no program. If this is not done, the whole range of programs would have to be repeated to get the desired results even though only one or two may have actually contributed to the desired outcome.

Another problem that plagues researchers and often prevents meaningful results from emerging is that the researcher is usually dependent on others for his input material. For example, the use of community informants such as professionals, relatives, friends, or the patients themselves frequently means that some information is lost. Every effort should be made to minimize this loss of follow-up data. The researcher should let the patient and the informant know that follow-up information will be requested and should maintain close contact with them. He should obtain the names and addresses of persons with stable addresses who will know the future whereabouts of the research subjects and help the investigator locate the ones who have moved.

The later community adjustment of hospital-treated schizophrenic patients can be assessed just as validly and reliably by patients' relatives as by professional staff, according to studies by Ellsworth et al. (1968) in which relatives completed questionnaires describing the expatient's behavior. Patients' relatives have much richer sources of data than does the staff upon which to base ratings, for the relatives typically observe what a patient says and does for several hours each day.

Thus far we have presented some of the problems in evalu-

165

ating programs and some of the means for making research more meaningful. What about gaining a better understanding of the treatment process itself? Do we know what really works? Is it the treatment method? The relationship with a therapist? What makes a patient get better? Would he still improve if he were not in treatment at all? The thorny issue of the waiting list is a case in point.

Many public mental health facilities have more applicants than they can accept for service at the time the request for service is made. Such applicants usually are put on a waiting list. Often, when the name on the top of the waiting list is reached, weeks or months later, the applicant says, "Thanks very much, but I no longer need your help. I'm doing fine." This superficial telephone contact suggests the possibility that about the same proportion of waiting list patients as treatment patients improves.

A study by Saenger (1970) sheds light on this issue. He did a one-year-after-intake follow-up on more than a thousand patients from twenty-four mental health clinics in New York State. He presents evidence in his paper for summarizing that: "Among patients with a poor prognosis the treated recovered more often than untreated patients. Among those with a good prognosis, in contrast, the untreated tended to improve more often than treated patients." In the discussion of his findings he says: "If further research with randomly assigned patients should substantiate our findings, it would suggest that clinics might be well advised to devote more of their efforts to those cases they tend to consider poor treatment risks, rather than patients with a good chance of recovery even without treatment."

It may be that many emotional disturbances are self-limiting, like the common cold. It is generally agreed that a cold sufferer is likely to get over his symptoms in a few days, whether he consults a physician, or treats himself with aspirin, liquids, and bed rest, or tries to ignore his symptoms and continue his normal work routine as best he can.

All people experience changes in mood. Some people seek professional help when they are depressed or anxious. When such a person reaches a therapist in what may be a low point in his mood cycle, the therapist intervenes with psychotherapy and, perhaps, medication. If, after an interval, the patient is no longer depressed or anxious, both the therapist and patient attribute the improvement to treatment. It may be that what is at work is simply the normal mood change. Much more evaluation research than we have at present is needed in order to draw conclusions about the effectiveness of treatment.

Utilizing Research

The obvious reason for conducting evaluation studies is to get objective information to use as a guide for program development by the agency being studied and by other agencies. The chances of research findings' being used are enhanced if three conditions prevail: staff is actively involved in the study; research is initiated in response to a felt need of the agency; and there is rapid reporting of research findings. It is most important that the staff be involved in all phases of the study from the beginning to its completion, including the formulation of the specific questions to be answered, the data gathering phase, and the interpretation of the meaning and the implications of the results. Only in this way does the staff feel that it has a stake in the research and cooperate fully. Because of staff turnover, this process of sustaining interest and involvement is a continuous one. Time must be taken to inform new staff members of the history and current status of the research. Without the cooperation of staff it is impossible for the researcher to obtain the material he needs. Therefore, throughout the study, the researcher must inform the clinical staff of what he is doing and why he is doing it.

The research study most likely to be used in program development is one based on an immediate felt need of the agency such as a rapid initial project aimed at helping to solve an acute crisis. Clinical decisions often must be made quickly, based on data the researcher feels are inadequate. Nevertheless, rapid action research procedures still provide data more reliable than subjective impressions. The data are useful if they answer questions satisfactorily. Also, after the rapid initial project, the investigator is in a better position than he was initially, both because of his acceptance by the agency and because of the knowledge and experience he has gained, to follow up with a long-term project with a methodology leading to more reliable and valid data.

There are at least two levels on which to evaluate the success of a demonstration project. The obvious level is in terms of developing an effective functioning model—that is, how well does the demonstration project work? This is the usual criterion. The second measure of success is the extent to which the model continues to be used after the demonstration project has been completed. This second criterion is related to the problem of research utilization and the planning for change. It is naive to believe that if the researcher creates a successful working model it will be automatically adopted as standard operating procedure. People strongly resist changing their practices. The working model has a better chance of being continued if staff shares in and has a voice in deciding each change as it occurs, during and following the research period, than if staff is excluded.

A study I directed in a state institution is an example of a demonstration project which was a success on level one, creating an effective working model, but was a failure on level two, having the model followed after the demonstration project was completed. A primary goal of the study was to change the way in which patients' work assignments were used from serving the needs of the institution to serving the rehabilitative needs of the patient. In organizational terms this meant moving industrial therapy assignments from the custodial-maintenance continuum to the treatment-rehabilitation continuum. The bakery was utilized for this portion of the study, not as a setting in which to train patients to become bakers in the community but as a work adjustment setting. This study is reported in considerable detail by Black (1970).

As long as the demonstration project was active and a research staff member worked with the bakers and patients, the bakery functioned as a work adjustment setting in accordance with the new model created by the study. Once adequate work habits were acquired, patient-workers were moved out of the bakery and out of the hospital into the community phase of the rehabilitation project model. When the project ended and the researchers were withdrawn, the bakers did not assume responsibility for maintaining the work adjustment atmosphere. Why not? My guess is that the project staff members were the ones who developed and maintained the work adjustment atmosphere and made the decisions, without sufficiently encouraging the bakers to assume new therapeutic responsibilities or involving them in the planning. For example, the counselor maintained contact with ward personnel regarding patient attendance at work and, often, did not encourage the bakers to develop this relationship with the ward staff. Thus the traditional work habits of the bakers did not have to change, and when the project ended, they were not prepared to take over the new ways.

Similarly, if a greater attempt had been made to involve other hospital departments in the ongoing functioning of the project, the chances of the new model's being continued would have been increased. In their eagerness to develop a successful model, the researchers quickly acceded to the wishes of hospital staff and assumed responsibility for the patients' adjustment to the program. The likelihood of the model's being used after the project ended would have been increased if the project staff had worked more persistently through existing hospital channels rather than by creating its own channels. Had this been done, perhaps the model would not have been as good a model—fewer patients would have been rehabilitated during the demonstration period—but more of the model would have become a part of normal operating procedures.

Negative Results

When a controlled study is conducted, there is usually resistance to publishing findings which are not favorable to the agency. Unfavorable or negative findings are those which show no statistically significant outcome differences between those getting agency services and those not getting such services, or which show that those getting agency services do not do as well. All kinds of "valid" reasons may be found for not disseminating the results. Most common is the objection that the agency has changed its methods and practices since the data were gathered and that therefore it would be unfair to publish them "now." Sometimes, to soften the effect of a research finding showing that an agency in fact does not achieve its objectives, the research report itself includes a statement to the effect that "these problems at the agency have already been corrected since the data were gathered." If the researcher is an employee of the agency, he is in a tight bind. He may have to choose between professional integrity and "loyalty" to his employer.

It is preferable that the researcher be an outsider, possibly with a university affiliation, and that he also have a genuine interest in the agency program and in program evaluation. However, he must be completely familiar with the agency and its procedures and he must receive all information known to insiders. Ideally, he should work closely with another researcher who is part of the organization.

But even an outsider finds his independence threatened if he reports negative findings. In the process of doing the study he develops personal relationships with the staff members and tends to find himself emotionally involved with them and their program efforts. In addition to his reluctance to offend his friends, he fears losing his research affiliation. When it becomes known that the researcher has published findings not complimentary to one agency, he is not likely to be asked to serve as research consultant to other agencies, even though his university colleagues may have applauded him and his academic career may have been advanced. Also, publishing is important to a researcher and journal editors prefer to publish research evaluation papers based on statistically significant differences between experimental and control groups. The net result is that papers reporting no differences between treatment and nontreatment groups rarely are published. When they are published, the findings are usually muted. Success stories are preferred to stories of failure.

Even when a rehabilitation agency is genuinely interested in evaluating its effectiveness and cooperates in a controlled study, there are still difficulties. One well functioning, prestigious social-vocational rehabilitation agency for psychiatric patients conducted a two-year experimental study involving some four hundred recently released mental hospital patients who applied to it for rehabilitation services. The goal was to provide some definitions of the role of the agency in the rehabilitation process of its clients. Assignment to one of four groups was made strictly by rotation at the time of application. Each of the three experimental groups received a different predetermined rehabilitation experience. The fourth was a control group which was not accepted into the agency at all.

The control group was used as the basis for evaluating the overall impact of the service. The differential effect of the various programs was to be evaluated by comparing the outcomes of the three experimental groups with each other.

Briefly, Group I clients were assigned to a social worker who established contact with the patient immediately after application. The social worker made an initial evaluation of the former patient's needs, worked closely with him over a two year period, and gradually involved him in the areas of the program of the rehabilitation center and in the facilities in the community which the worker felt were indicated. Emphasis was placed on the development of a significant relationship between the worker and the client as a way of involving in the program clients who otherwise would drop out. It was hypothesized that this would be the most effective and successful program.

Group II clients also were assigned to a worker who established contact with the expatient immediately after application. However, the professional worked with the client for only one month, attempting to involve him in those areas of the agency program which he felt were appropriate to his needs. After the one-month period, the client no longer received special attention and his use of agency facilities was completely optional. As was true of non-research clients, further relationship with staff depended upon efforts of the client.

Group III clients from the start were not followed closely by any staff worker, and participation in the program and relationship with staff was on a completely optional basis for these clients, as it was for nonresearch clients. Their program resembled the original, inexpensive program of the agency, simply providing a clubhouse and activities for expatients who chose to use it.

Group IV served as controls. These applicants were not accepted into the program.

The individuals in all four research groups were evaluated every three months, regardless of their participation in the agency program. The evaluation focused upon rehospitalization, vocational adjustment, and use of facilities outside the agency being studied.

The data obtained in the study showed, among other findings, that the rehospitalization rates of the three experimental groups combined were consistently lower—at every three-month interval in the study—than were the rates for the control group; this percentage difference was statistically significant for the six- and nine-month-in-study intervals. These results were presented at a national professional meeting and were subsequently published in a professional journal. However, the data did not show the expected differences between the three experimental groups. It was anticipated that Group I would have the lowest rehospitalization rate. There were in fact no significant differences in rehospitalization rates among the three experimental groups. These negative results were not published. The published paper reported "preliminary findings" and included a statement that future reports would explore the question: "Do the three different rehabilitative programs for the experimental groups differ in their effectiveness?" Actually there was considerable resistance to publishing the negative findings; eleven years after the data were gathered nothing has been published comparing the effectiveness of the three experimental groups.

In effect, the total program for Group I had already been evaluated by a number of subjective "measures" before the controlled study was undertaken, and it was found to be successful. These subjective measures included: a feeling of satisfaction by the professionals involved in the program; an increasing number of persons seeking services from the agency; an absence of complaints; and a feeling by the board of directors, supporting private foundations and government agencies, and the individual contributors that the agency was doing a good job. All of this resulted in a rapidly increasing annual budget and a proliferation of programs. When all is going so well, why look into research data that might question the effectiveness of the many-faceted and expensive program developed by the agency over the years?

To these surprise and dismay of the agency staff, the research seemed to indicate that the original economical program of providing a clubhouse for expatients who chose to use it was as effective in increasing community tenure and level of social and vocational functioning as was the elaborate experimental program involving many and varied programs and professional counselors who reached out to those patients who did not use the program on their own. But by ignoring or rationalizing away the negative findings, the professional staff could comfortably continue expanding its program, persisting in the belief that it is valuable; they had salved their scientific conscience by publishing a "preliminary report" which shows that the agency program is more effective than no program. Their belief in the value of what they are doing permits them to postpone indefinitely an examination of the data relating to the effectiveness or lack of effectiveness of the new elaborate program as compared to the simple voluntary program out of which it had been developed.

A Positive Note

We have seen that most programs in mental health and rehabilitation are not evaluated in a scientific way. We have emphasized the need in conducting research for administrative support at all levels and the need for controlled studies. We have noted the problems associated with doing such studies, problems in research utilization and in making research meaningful, and the resistances to publishing negative research findings.

Sometimes negative research results do get published and even lead to the development of new and different approaches to treatment. Good controlled research programs can be conducted by independent researchers, even within large bureaucratic hospitals.

173

Fairweather and Simon (1963) in such manner found many hospital programs were effective in getting patients out of the hospital but did not significantly reduce recidivism. He found that patients who received individual psychotherapy or group psychotherapy or who lived and worked together as groups were making no better or worse community adjustment eighteen months after release from the hospital than those patients who had simply participated in the regular hospital program. Very little relationship was found between improvement in the hospital and subsequent adjustment to community living. Further, regardless of treatment, seventy-two per cent of the chronic psychotic patients returned to the hospital within eighteen months of their release.

It was decided that new treatment programs should be devised for those patients who were spending most of their lives in the mental hospital. (Fairweather's program is described in some detail in Chapter Five.) Briefly, the next step was to attempt to set up a ward composed of patients who planned their own futures. It was found that such small groups of patients whose daily activities were organized around solving their own problems could be formed by even the most chronically ill patients and that the patients could take care of each other and successfully handle their daily problems. These problem-solving groups worked very well in the hospital: patients assumed a great deal of autonomy, patient and staff morale increased, and patients completed their treatment program much more quickly than did those on the traditional ward. But despite all these benefits, once a patient left the hospital and his reference group, he returned to the hospital as quickly as did a person who had participated in the traditional program. There was a very high relationship between a patient's remaining in the community and the support he received from the people with whom he lived. This later research finding suggested that if the group itself could be moved into the community as a unit, it might provide such a supportive situation.

A study to test this hypothesis was undertaken in which chronic mental patients were divided into two groups. Both participated in the small group problem-solving hospital treatment program, but when the time came to leave the hospital the experimentals left for a community dormitory (lodge) where a work and living situation was provided for them while the controls left the hospital independently and used the regular treatment facilities available for expatients in the community.

The results were most impressive. As described in Chapter Five, these ex-mental patients eventually became entirely autonomous and self-supporting. During the first six months of follow-up, sixty-five per cent of those who went to the dormitory remained in the community at least seventy-five per cent of the time whereas only twenty-four per cent of those receiving traditional community services remained outside as long. Fifty per cent of those who went to the dormitory were employed at least seventy-five per cent of the time while only three per cent of those receiving the usual community treatment were employed as long. These differences for the first six months were not transitory. Similar differences continued throughout the entire forty-month follow-up period of the project.

And the reduction in cost was dramatic. The community treatment program costs less than half of that of hospital care. But reduced costs do not convey the high morale of the dormitory members and their generally improved perception of themselves and others. The improvement in the ex-mental patients' perception of themselves and their world was heartening for all mental health workers associated with the project.

Despite these dramatic results, Fairweather and his co-workers (1970) were not content merely to publish their findings. Continuing to function within a research framework, they have developed a program to help other mental hospitals develop community treatment programs of this type. Fairweather's activities are cited to indicate what can happen with the kind of scientific assessment talked about in this chapter.

In some ways the role of the clinician appears to be incompatible with the role of the researcher. The clinician must have faith in the value of what he is doing and must convey this faith to the client. The researcher, on the other hand, approaches his task with a questioning attitude. He is skeptical, dispassionate, and objective.

175

But this apparent incompatibility of roles must be seen in a different perspective. Often there is lack of clarity within the agency with respect to the broadest aspects of treatment goals—for example, reduction of specific symptoms vs. insight; competitive employment vs. social rehabilitation. Not infrequently, the discussion between clinicians and program evaluators for the purpose of formulating criteria of success of the planned study leads to a clarification of the agency's goals.

It is a cliché to say today that research and service go hand in hand. Ideally, they do. The clinician needs the researcher's objective support for his practices and the researcher needs the clinician's insights in formulating his research questions. Better research and better clinical practice result from cooperation between the two.

Epilogue

H. Richard Lamb, Victor Goertzel

W_e have sought to show that rehabilitation of the psychiatric patient builds upon a number of basic concepts. The practical application of these concepts is not an easy matter, however, and we are painfully conscious of an ongoing process of trial and error. But we can learn from the experience of others, as demonstrated by the examples cited in this book.

The basic concepts to which we refer appear in all phases of rehabilitation, whether social or vocational. For instance, placing the focus on changing behavior, while leaving basic personality structure alone, is an integral part of the philosophy of rehabilitation counseling, of the sheltered workshop and sheltered work placements, of life habit training in the halfway house, and of all forms of social rehabilitation. The same is true with respect to a related concept, that of working with and trying to expand the well part of the personality rather than being primarily concerned with pathology.

Maintaining expectations that people live up to their potential, however high or low that potential may be, applies equally well to work, to the ability to live independently or semi-independently, and to the ability to derive satisfaction from relationships with others. We have seen the importance of taking into account individual differences in people; we must not expect the same degree of competence from everyone but must be flexible while maintaining high expectations.

We must strive to minimize labeling and stigmatization of people as mentally ill. Many persons disabled by the kinds of behavior called mental illness need to begin their rehabilitation programs in segregated facilities such as day treatment centers, sheltered workshops, halfway houses, and expatient clubs. But these facilities should be seen as transitional. The next step is to less segregated settings like sheltered work placements, satellite housing, and social placement programs such as the one developed at Thresholds. Ideally, the client will reach competitive employment, independent living, and use of the regular social and recreational resources of the community. Throughout, the high expectation approach emphasizes to him his strengths and assures him that society regards him not simply as a mental patient but as a person with avenues of social and vocational achievement open to him. Thus he is less likely to be stigmatized as mentally ill by himself or by others.

If a person is not capable of using nonsegregated facilities, it is better that he use a segregated service than none at all. Though the emphasis in rehabilitation is on the transitional period, many persons need long-term or even permanent sheltered work, living, and social facilities. We in rehabilitation must find ways of meeting this need. One of the basic assumptions of the transitional workshop is that it makes an important contribution when it prepares persons who are incapable of competitive employment for long-term sheltered employment. Likewise, the satellite housing concept allows persons to make their permanent homes in housing units with varying degrees of supervision.

Epilogue

Does this body of knowledge have applications in other fields of rehabilitation? Obviously it does apply in rehabilitation of the physically disabled, from which much of this knowledge has been drawn. Rehabilitation workers also have made important contributions toward meeting the needs of the culturally disadvantaged (see Chapters Three and Five). But there is another group for which large-scale rehabilitation efforts are just getting underway and to which much of the experience with the mentally ill can be directly applied. We are referring to exconvicts and to the vast number of persons still in prison. There has been speculation that the status of prisons today is comparable to that of state hospitals fifteen years ago and that development of community resources will lead to a mass exodus from the prisons (Tyce, 1971).

A close look at the prison population reveals many similarities to the mentally ill. A high proportion of offenders are characterized by lack of ego strength. They are unable to cope with the demands of the outside world, an inadequacy which is compounded by their lack of impulse control and inability to tolerate anxiety or frustration. If one of the usual crises of life arises while they are in the community, they need immediate help to deal with it. Crisis intervention is equally as important for exconvicts as for the mentally ill, if they are to remain in the community.

Convicts are dependent on a total institution, the prison, and are just as institutionalized as are the long-term mentally ill in state hospitals. Going directly from the protected environment of prison to independent living is too often a formula for failure. Clearly, exconvicts, too, need the supportive living arrangements like halfway houses and supervised apartment programs described in Chapter Six.

Vocational rehabilitation services are also crucial for the exconvict. Not only must he have a job, but it must be one suited to him. Rehabilitation counseling is necessary, not only in the vocational evaluation and job finding phases, but while he is adjusting to the demands of employment.

The target populations are being identified, and methods of rehabilitation are being developed to deal with their problems.

But funds must be made available for a large-scale expansion of vocational rehabilitation services, including sheltered workshops and other sheltered work arrangements, and for sheltered living arrangements which foster rehabilitation and prevent regression. More attention must be paid to evaluation, so that programs are developed from objective study rather than from subjective impressions, and community mental health facilities must be available to support these programs with crisis intervention, medications, and the alternative of brief hospitalization in community facilities rather than in a state hospital. They should also provide consultation to such social agencies as welfare departments, boarding homes, probation departments, and the police.

Meeting the needs of the mentally ill, the culturally disadvantaged, and the exconvict population constitutes some of our most pressing social problems. Reassessment of our national priorities must not only recognize this problem but also lead to a decision to allocate more of our resources than we do at present to finding solutions. Rehabilitation techniques and skills, and the concepts on which they are based, can play a leading role in the remedy of these social ills.

Role of the Workshop Foreman

❋⳹❋⳹❋⳹❋⳹❋⳹❋⳹❋⳹❋⳹❋⳹❋⳹❋⳹❋⳹❋⳹❋⳹❋

This guide stems from the need to define the job of a foreman in the structure of a workshop. There is considerable debate in the rehabilitation workshop movement about who should be hired for the job of foreman. Some agencies insist upon professionally trained, psychologically oriented people, while others stoutly maintain that the role should be filled by industrially trained people skilled in production. We feel that the most practical way to shed light on this problem is to detail as carefully as possible what the job actually entails.

Foreman-Client Relationship

The key relationship in the workshop is that between the foreman and the client. The client-foreman relationship is work-centered and directed toward challenging the client to expend more energy on work, to learn how to work effectively, and to eliminate

181

inappropriate work behavior. The relationship is, to a large extent, nonverbal (as described in some detail in Chapter Three) and ranges in tone from supportive to authoritarian.

It is important for foreman and client to have good rapport. But the foreman must guard against overidentification with the client. He must avoid a social relationship with clients and keep the focus on what he and the client together are working to accomplish. He functions neither as a counselor nor as a social worker but in his own role as work supervisor. The relationship must remain a businesslike one, unhindered by considerations of friendship and emotional overinvolvement. It must approximate as nearly as possible the relationship existing in industry between foremen and workers.

The foreman has the key role in orienting the client toward seeing the workshop as simulating a genuine work situation. Staff can take elaborate steps to convince clients that the workshop is neither a school nor an institution, but the necessary atmosphere for evaluation is not offered unless the foreman is seen by the client as the line authority on output. The foreman insists on product quality and appropriate work behavior. However, since he also must be aware of the rehabilitation aspects of the workshop, he must be constantly alert to the client's area of need at the moment in order to help him move toward a vocational goal.

In the day-to-day contact, the foreman confronts the client with the reality of his performance—be it quality of product or manner of behavior—so that the client has honest, specific feedback on his performance and can start on a reality-based program of dealing with problems. Hostility, aggression, or withdrawal as a response to confrontation does not cause the foreman to overreact or withdraw; rather, by his handling these reactions in a mature way, with understanding, he models the kind of behavior he wants his clients to learn.

Observation of Client

The foreman's first contact is assignment of the client to his job. He observes the client's learning pattern, use of energies and abilities, attention span, and handling of materials. In the initial and succeeding contacts he is sensitive to the client's ability to utilize supervision and to the client's interaction with co-workers. He gauges the client's degree of gratification from work, self-concept as a worker, and ability to adjust to challenge and to grasp the purpose of his being in the workshop.

Attitude Toward Clients

Unless the foreman is able to recognize the essential value and dignity of each of the clients under his supervision, he will not be able to establish an atmosphere conducive to rehabilitation. The expectations he places on his clients, by not doing for them but helping them learn to do for themselves, imply their ability to improve. Neither paternalism nor unduly harsh demands are helpful in the process.

Quality Control

The foreman has frequent contact with the client to instruct, demonstrate, or display methods of work. He checks regularly on the hour or half-hour for adherence to the proper method of work, for output, and for quality. Quality is stressed, and only after it has been established does the foreman press for quantity in production. Having established the proper quality, he seeks to challenge the client by pointing out the industrial rate of production. He notes the rejects and subtracts them from the total amount produced.

In addition to the importance of quality as it contributes to the client's rehabilitation is the consideration of meeting customers' specifications. The foremen are responsible for the quality of work that leaves the shop. Seeing the foreman's serious attention to this cannot help but impress upon the client the importance of quality.

Work Habits

The foreman corrects lapses in work behavior such as lateness, poor work posture, unnecessary motions, resistance to supervision, talking too much, and so on. He enforces workshop rules about when to call in about illness, use of the telephone, and appropriate behavior toward other clients and staff. By this method he helps the clients to establish proper habits of work.

Manipulation of Work Environment

The foreman also challenges the client by manipulating work content and environment. He may move the client from one kind of work to another, or he may keep the client on the same job for a long time. He may move the client from an individual to a group job. He may find a more complex job to test the client's ability or step up pressures to see if the client can tolerate more of them. In making all of these changes, the foreman follows a prior plan which has been worked out off the floor. All the while, the foreman carefully records his notes so that he does not have to rely on memory for facts about important reactions that took place on the work floor.

Responsibility for Contracts

The foreman receives instruction on methods and standards of production from the chief foreman. Before teaching a client, the foreman must know the job operations involved. He prepares the layout of the work materials and sees that all is in readiness for the client to work, including precount of the materials. He reports to the chief foreman all materials needed to complete the work. Frequently the foreman is assigned responsibility for a subcontract, in which case he must know production schedules, control the flow and quality of materials, and maintain an accurate inventory. This requires careful coordination with the chief foreman and the procurement officer. Sometimes the foreman is called upon to work with other staff to devise jigs and to work out time-saving production methods.

Recording

Each foreman must have at least forty minutes daily to record his observations and impressions so that staff receives a coherent, factual, and well organized account of client behavior, including measurements of productivity.

Planning Meeting

Each afternoon (client's coffee break) there is a brief planning meeting to assign clients to the next day's work. This meeting gives the foreman a chance to raise special problems and to work out the specific assignments suitable for the client. Of particular importance is the opportunity to check on whether the plan for the client is being followed or needs modification.

Evaluation

At the biweekly evaluation of each client, progress is reviewed: his assets and liabilities are described in relation to employability. In most instances the client and his rehabilitation counselor should be present. The client benefits from hearing a frank discussion of his progress (or lack of it) and the evaluation does not take on the character of a closed-door session held behind his back. At the evaluation, the foreman presents his observations of performance, highlighting the cogent aspects of the client's work personality. He estimates the client's readiness to move from the shop and makes suggestions about what he needs to work on to enhance his progress.

In such an open meeting, the client can be truly involved in his own rehabilitation plan and has the opportunity to confront the foreman with any observations he feels are incorrect or unfair. The foreman must be able to deal with such confrontation in a fair, helpful manner.

The quality of a foreman's work is reflected in the evaluation. A good evaluation is the product of close supervision, intelligent challenge to the client, intense observation, and specificity of description so that clichés and stereotypes are not substituted for individualized views of the client's particular personality.

Relationship to Supervision and Referring Agencies

The foreman must have ability to work within an organizational framework; this implies the ability to follow instructions and to utilize supervision. Meetings with outside personnel are part of the program, usually related to evaluation. However, responsibility goes beyond mutual interest in a client; it requires that the service be interpreted to the agencies, that they be familiarized with workshop structure, and introduced, many for the first time, to a technique for evaluation in an actual work setting.

Workshops serve clients referred by rehabilitation counselors so that, in a sense, counselors are their primary "customers." Since the foreman deals directly with his clients, the counselor looks to him for ongoing assessment of the client's progress and for carrying out a rehabilitation plan. The foreman must be able to communicate with counselors in a meaningful way and be willing and able to enter into a cooperative relationship with them. The foreman must recognize and accept that the counselor has the overall responsibility for the client's rehabilitation. The counselor has more knowledge about the client in aspects outside of the workshop than the foreman has. Sometimes he may want certain specific services or ask that some things be avoided. Sometimes his requests are puzzling to the foreman, who sees the client only in one setting. The foreman must be flexible enough to cooperate with the counselor, bearing in mind that the goal for him, as well as for the counselor, is the most effective way of rehabilitating the client.

Attitude to Work

The foreman's own attitude to work is his most important contribution. If he sees himself as a producer and focuses his energy on work, he transmits his concentration to the client. If he gets satisfaction from the physical, psychological, and social aspects of his work, he transmits this satisfaction. By means of his own work habits, self-discipline, and concern for standards, he sets an example for the client.

For the foreman, the feeling that he has done meaningful work arises from two factors. First, the foreman gains satisfaction in creating an atmosphere which directs his client's energy toward work and rehabilitation. A second source of satisfaction is the actual physical production of the subcontract. Being identified with the mainstream of the economy through productivity is transmitted to the client as a positive and gratifying feeling.

If they lose sight of the importance of the production of things, workshops tend to become clinics rather than work adjustment centers. But if they lose sight of the main problems—the relations between people—they become factories with the goal of production rather than the improvement of people. Thus, the foreman needs to perceive himself as a producer of a service *and* a producer of things; the challenge for him is to achieve the delicate balance between serving clients' rehabilitation needs and serving the production needs of contracts. If a workshop achieves this balance, it is neither a clinic nor a factory but, rather, a place where production is used to rehabilitate people.

Attitude Toward Placement

For a workshop, giving good technical services is not enough. The goal is to prepare people for real jobs outside the shop. This means that the foreman must feel some real urgency in seeing clients make the internal gains which spell movement toward a job. If he forgets that his client's main goal is a job in the outside world, with its rewards and its difficulties, the foreman can become sterile or overclinical in his work. Even though he does not enter directly into the placement function, he must be aware of the demands of a real job in order to help the client and the placement officer find the most realistic place for the client in the world of work.

Bibliography

ABROMS, G. M. "Defining Milieu Therapy." *Archives of General Psychiatry,* 1969, *21,* 553–560.

Action for Mental Health, final report of the Joint Commission on Mental Illness and Health. New York: Basic Books, 1961.

APTE, R. Z. *Halfway Houses: A New Dilemma in Institutional Care.* London: G. Bell and Sons, 1968.

BACHMAN, B. J. "Re-entering the Community: A Former Patient's View," *Hospital and Community Psychiatry,* 1971, 22, 119–122.

BARTON, E. *The Rehabilitation Workshop Foreman and His Role.* San Francisco: Rehabilitation Workshop Administration, University of San Francisco, 1971.

BARTON, E., AND BARTON, E. *The Requirements of Effective Sheltered Workshop Supervision,* final report of research grant 1182. Washington, D.C.: Vocational Rehabilitation Administration, Department of Health, Education, and Welfare, 1965.

BEARD, J. H., GOERTZEL, V., AND PEARCE, A. J. "The Effectiveness of Activity Group Therapy with Chronically Regressed Adult

189

Bibliography

Schizophrenics." *International Journal of Group Psychotherapy,*
1958, *8,* 123–136.

BEARD, J. H., PITT, R. B., FISHER, S. H., AND GOERTZEL, V. "Evaluating
the Effectiveness of a Psychiatric Rehabilitation Program."
American Journal of Orthopsychiatry, 1963, *33,* 701–712.

BEARD, J. H., SCHMIDT, J. R., AND SMITH, M. M. "The Use of Transitional Employment in the Rehabilitation of the Psychiatric Patient." *Journal of Nervous and Mental Disease,* 1963, *136,* 507–
514.

BEARD, J. H., SCHMIDT, J. R., SMITH, M. M., AND DINCIN, J. "Three Aspects of Psychiatric Rehabilitation at Fountain House." *Mental
Hygiene,* 1964, *48,* 11–21.

BENJAMIN, A. *The Helping Interview.* Boston: Houghton Mifflin, 1969.

BIERER, J. "A Survey of Social Club Therapy." In J. Bierer (Ed.),
Therapeutic Social Clubs. London: H. K. Lewis, 1948.

BLACK, B. J. *Principles of Industrial Therapy for the Mentally Ill.* New
York: Grune and Stratton, 1970.

BOROW, H. *Man in a World at Work.* Boston: Houghton Mifflin, 1964.

BRIGHT, J. R. "The Relationship of Increasing Automation and Skill
Requirements." In National Commission on Technology, Auto-
mation, and Economic Progress, *The Employment Impact of
Technological Change,* Appendix Vol. 2: Technology and the
American Economy. Washington: Government Printing Office,
1966.

Brochure of Transitional Services, Inc. Pittsburgh: June 1970.

BURCK, G. "There'll Be Less Leisure Than You Think." *Fortune,*
March 1970, 87–89.

BUTTON, W. B. (Ed.) *Rehabilitation, Sheltered Workshops and the Disadvantaged.* Ithaca: New York State School of Industrial and
Labor Relations, Cornell University, 1970.

CARSTAIRS, G. M. "A Land of Lotus-Eaters?" *American Journal of
Psychiatry,* 1969, *125,* 1576–1580.

CARTER, R. "The Myth of Increasing Non-Work vs. Work Activities."
Social Problems, 1970, *18,* 52–67.

COHEN, A., AND ORZECH, D. *A Study of the Feasibility for Vocational
Rehabilitation of a Perplexing Group of Mental Hospital Patients,* final report of research and demonstration RD-505. De-
troit: Social and Rehabilitation Service, Department of Health,
Education, and Welfare, 1970.

CONLEY, R. *The Economics of Vocational Rehabilitation.* Baltimore:
Johns Hopkins Press, 1965.

DINCIN, J., AND SWIFT, J. W. *The Post-Hospital Schizophrenic Patient,*
final report of research and demonstration project 1058-P.

Chicago: Social and Rehabilitation Service, Department of Health, Education, and Welfare, 1967.

DUMONT, M. P. "Industrial Psychiatry for the Employer of Last Resort." *Community Mental Health Journal*, 1970, *6*, 411–417.

ELLSWORTH, R. B., FOSTER, L., CHILDERS, B., ARTHUR, G., AND KROEKER, D. "Hospital and Community Adjustment as Perceived by Psychiatric Patients, Their Families, and Staff." *Journal of Consulting and Clinical Psychology* (Monograph), 1968, *32*, No. 5, Part 2.

ELLUL, J. "Reflections on Leisure." *Reflections*, 1968, *3*, 1–15.

FAIRWEATHER, G. W. *Social Psychology in Treating Mental Illness*. New York: Wiley, 1964.

FAIRWEATHER, G. W., SANDERS, D. H., MAYNARD, H., AND CRESSLER, D. L. *Community Life for the Mentally Ill: An Alternative to Institutional Care*. Chicago: Aldine, 1969.

FAIRWEATHER, G. W., AND SIMON, R. "A Further Follow-up Comparison of Psychotherapeutic Programs." *Journal of Consulting Psychology*, 1963, *27*, 186.

FORD, R. M. "The Obstinate Employee." *Psychology Today*, November 1969, *3*, 32–35.

FREEMAN, H. E., AND SIMMONS, O. G. *The Mental Patient Comes Home*. New York: Wiley, 1963.

FRIEDSON, E. "Disability as Social Deviance." In Sussman, M. B. (Ed.), *Sociology and Rehabilitation*. Washington, D.C.: American Sociological Association, 1965.

GELLMAN, W., GENDEL, H., GLASER, N. M., FRIEDMAN, S. B., AND NEFF, W. S. *Adjusting People to Work*. Chicago: Jewish Vocational Services, Monograph No. 1, 1957.

GLASSCOTE, R. M., CUMMING, E., RUTMAN, I., SUSSEX, J. N., AND GLASSMAN, S. M. *Rehabilitating the Mentally Ill in the Community*. Washington, D.C.: Joint Information Service of American Psychiatric Association and National Association for Mental Health, 1971.

GLASSCOTE, R. M., GUDEMAN, J. E., AND ELPERS, R. *Halfway Houses for the Mentally Ill*. Washington, D.C.: Joint Information Service of American Psychiatric Association and National Association for Mental Health, 1971.

GOERTZEL, V. "Evaluation of Halfway House Programs for Returned Mental Patients." *The Quarterly of Camarillo*, 1965, *1*, 5–15.

GOERTZEL, V., BEARD, J. H., AND PILNICK, S. "Fountain House Foundation: Case Study of an Expatients' Club." *Journal of Social Issues*, 1960, *16*, 54–61.

GOFFMAN, E. *Asylums*. Garden City, N.Y.: Doubleday, 1961.

Bibliography

GOODE, W. J. "The Protection of the Inept." *American Sociological Review,* 1967, *32,* 5–19.

GOVEIA, H., AND TUTKO, T. A. *Psychiatric Rehabilitation in a Community Center,* final report of United States Public Health Service research grant MH 01531, National Institute of Mental Health. Santa Clara, Calif.: Rehabilitation Mental Health Services, 1969.

HAUN, P. "Leisure." In Martin, P. A. (Ed.), *Leisure and Mental Health: A Psychiatric Viewpoint.* Washington, D.C.: American Psychiatric Association, 1967.

HAVIGHURST, R. J. "Youth in Exploration and Man Emergent." In H. Borow (Ed.), *Man in a World of Work.* Boston: Houghton Mifflin, 1964.

HAWKER, A. "Are Hospitals Really Necessary—Setting Up the House." *Alcoholism, 3,* 1966, 183–186.

HERZBERG, F. "One More Time: How Do You Motivate Employees?" *Harvard Business Review,* January–February 1968, 53–62.

HERZBERG, F., MAUSNER, B., AND SNYDERMAN, B. B. *The Motivation to Work.* New York: Wiley, 1959.

JONES, M. "Report on Social Psychiatry." In Wilmer, H. A. (Ed.), *Research Report.* Bethesda: Naval Medical Research Institute, 1958.

JONES, M. "The Current Place of Therapeutic Communities in Psychiatric Practice." In Freeman, H., and Farndale, J. (Eds.), *New Aspects of the Mental Health Services.* Oxford: Pergamon Press, 1967.

KORNHAUSER, A. *Mental Health of the Industrial Worker.* New York: Wiley, 1965.

KRUMBOLTZ, J. D. *Revolution in Counseling.* Boston: Houghton Mifflin, 1966.

LAMB, H. R. "Coordination: The Key to Rehabilitation." *Hospital and Community Psychiatry,* 1971, *22,* 46–47.

LAMB, H. R., AND GOERTZEL, V. "Discharged Patients—Are They Really in the Community." *Archives of General Psychiatry,* 1971, *24,* 29–34.

LAMB, H. R., AND MACKOTA, C. "Vocational Rehabilitation Services." In Lamb, H. R., Heath, D., and Downing, J. J. (Eds.), *Handbook of Community Mental Health Practice.* San Francisco: Jossey-Bass, 1969.

LANDY, D., AND GREENBLATT, M. *Halfway House: A Sociocultural and Clinical Study of Rutland Corner House, A Transitional Aftercare Residence for Female Psychiatric Patients.* Washington,

Bibliography

D.C.: Vocational Rehabilitation Administration, Department of Health, Education, and Welfare, 1965.

LECHT, L. A. *Manpower Needs for National Goals in the 1970's*. New York: Praeger, 1969.

LIPSITT, D. R. "Help and Overhelp." *Medical Opinion and Review,* 1968, *4,* 92–103.

LISS, S. S. *The Community Oriented Remotivation Program—CORP —A Progress Report.* Denver: Mimeographed, June 1969.

LUDWIG, A. M., AND FARRELLY, F. "The Code of Chronicity." *Archives of General Psychiatry,* 1966, *15,* 562–568.

MAISEL, R. "The Ex-Mental Patient and Rehospitalization: Some Research Findings." *Social Problems,* 1967, *15,* 18–24.

MALIKIN, D., AND RUSALEM, H. *Vocational Rehabilitation of the Disabled—An Overview.* New York: New York University Press, 1969.

MC DONOUGH, J. M. "The Veterans Administration and Community Mental Health: New Approaches in Psychiatric Rehabilitation." *Community Mental Health Journal,* 1969, *5,* 275–279.
nity Mental Health Journal, 1969, 5, 275–279.

MC GOWAN, J. F., AND SCHMIDT, L. D. *Counseling: Readings in Theory and Practice.* New York: Holt, Rinehart, and Winston, 1962.

MEYER, H. J., AND BORGATTA, E. F. *An Experiment in Mental Patient Rehabilitation: Evaluating a Social Agency Program.* New York: Russell Sage Foundation, 1959.

MILLER, D., DAWSON, W., AND BARNHOUSE, R. *Reconstruction of the Self: Toward a Theory of Social Rehabilitation,* final report of National Institute of Mental Health project MH 01646-03. San Francisco: Mimeographed, 1968.

MILLER, L. *Resource-Centered Counselor-Client Interaction in Rehabilitation Settings.* Iowa City: Mimeographed, 1966.

MUTH, L. T. *Community Treatment of Mental Illness: A World Survey.* Washington, D.C.: United States Public Health Service, Department of Health, Education, and Welfare, 1961.

NAGI, S. Z. "Some Conceptual Issues in Disability and Rehabilitation." In Sussman, M. B. (Ed.), *Sociology and Rehabilitation.* Washington, D.C.: American Sociological Association, 1965.

NEFF, W. S. *Work and Human Behavior.* New York: Atherton Press, 1968.

NIXON, R. A. "The Impact of Automation and Technological Change on the Employability of the Mentally Retarded," paper presented at the Annual Meeting of the American Academy on Mental Retardation. San Francisco: May 13, 1969.

Bibliography

Occupational Guide. Sacramento: California Department of Human Resources Development, 1970.

OLSHANSKY, S. "Some Assumptions Challenged." *Community Mental Health Journal,* 1968, *4,* 153–156.

PATTERSON, C. H. (Ed.) *Readings on Rehabilitation Counseling.* Champaign: Stiples, 1960.

PATTERSON, C. H. "Counseling: Self Clarification and the Helping Relationship." In Borow, H. (Ed.), *Man in a World of Work.* Boston: Houghton Mifflin, 1964.

PATTERSON, C. H. *Theories of Counseling and Psychotherapy.* New York: Harper, 1966.

RAUSH, H. R., AND RAUSH, C. L. *The Halfway House Movement: A Search for Sanity.* New York: Appleton-Century-Crofts, 1968.

RICHMOND, C. "Transitional Housing." In Lamb, H. R., Heath, D., and Downing, J. J. (Eds.), *Handbook of Community Mental Health Practice.* San Francisco: Jossey-Bass, 1969.

RICHMOND, C. "Expanding the Concepts of the Halfway House: A Satellite Housing Program." *The International Journal of Social Psychiatry, 16,* 1970, 96–102.

RUTMAN, I. D. "Establishing New Principles and Methods for Rehabilitating the Mentally Ill," paper presented at the Meeting of the Eastern Psychological Association. Atlantic City: April 3, 1970.

SAENGER, G. "Patterns of Change among 'Treated' and 'Untreated' Patients Seen in Psychiatric Community Mental Health Clinics." *Journal of Nervous and Mental Diseases,* 1970, *150,* 37–50.

SANDERS, R., SMITH, R. S., AND WEINMAN, B. S. *Chronic Psychoses and Recovery.* San Francisco: Jossey-Bass, 1967.

SCHEFF, T. J. *Being Mentally Ill: A Sociological Theory.* Chicago: Aldine, 1966.

SCHMIDT, J. R., NESSEL, J. J., AND MALAMUD, T. J. *An Evaluation of Rehabilitation Services and the Role of Industry in the Community Adjustment of Psychiatric Patients Following Hospitalization,* final report of demonstration grant Rd-1281-P. New York: Social and Rehabilitation Service, Department of Health, Education, and Welfare, 1969.

SILBERSTEIN, S. O. *A Survey of the Mental Health Functions of the Systems of Residential Home Care for the Mentally Ill and Retarded in the Sacramento Area.* Sacramento: Mimeographed, 1969.

TOWNSEND, O. H. "Vocational Rehabilitation and the Black Counselor: The Conventional Training Situation and the Battleground Across Town." *Journal of Rehabilitation,* 1970, *36,* 16–18.

TYCE, F. A. "PORT of Olmsted County, Minnesota; Community Rehabilitation for Legal Offenders." *Hospital and Community Psychiatry,* 1971, *22,* 74–78.

TYLER, L. *Work of the Counselor.* New York: Appleton-Century-Crofts, 1969.

WECHSLER, H. "Halfway Houses for Former Mental Patients: A Survey." *Journal of Social Issues,* 1960, *16,* 20–26.

WECHSLER, H. "The Ex-Patient Club: A General Survey and Case Study." In Greenblatt, M., Levinson, D. J., and Klerman, G. L. (Eds.), *Mental Patients in Transition.* Springfield, Ill.: Thomas, 1961.

WEINMAN, B., SANDERS, R., KLEINER, R., AND WILSON, S. "Community Based Treatment of the Chronic Psychotic." *Community Mental Health Journal,* 1970, *6,* 13–21.

WEISS, R. S., AND KAHN, R. L. *On the Evaluation of Work Among American Men.* Unpublished manuscript, 1959.

WILENSKY, H. L. "Varieties of Work Experience." In Borow, H. (Ed.), *Man in a World of Work.* Boston: Houghton Mifflin, 1964.

WILDER, J. F., KESSELL, M., AND CAULFIELD, S. C. "Follow-up of a 'High Expectations' Halfway House." *American Journal of Psychiatry,* 1968, *124,* 1085–1091.

WILMER, H. A., AND LAMB, H. R. "Using Therapeutic Community Principles." In Lamb, H. R., Heath, D., and Downing, J. J. (Eds.), *Handbook of Community Mental Health Practice.* San Francisco: Jossey-Bass, 1969.

WOLKON, G. H. "Characteristics of Clients and Continuity of Care into the Community." *Community Mental Health Journal,* 1970, *6,* 215–221.

WRIGHT, G. N., REAGLES, K. W., AND BUTLER, A. J. *The Wood County Project—Final Report.* Madison: University of Wisconsin Regional Rehabilitation Research Institute, 1969.

ZUSMAN, J. "A Rudimentary Guide to Social Therapies." *Hospital and Community Psychiatry,* 1969, *20,* 59–62.

Name Index

Name Index

Name Index

SANDERS, D. H., 139
SANDERS, R., 139, 153
SCHEFF, T. J., 8, 9, 10, 14
SCHMIDT, J. R., 96, 101, 160
SCHMIDT, L. D., 31
SILBERSTEIN, S. O., 6
SIMMONS, O. G., 4, 137
SIMON, R., 174
SMITH, M. M., 96, 160
SMITH, R. S., 139, 153
SNYDERMAN, B. B., 18
SUSSEX, J. N., 142
SWIFT, J. W., 24, 102, 149

T

TOWNSEND, O. H., 112
TUFKO, T. A., 126

TYCE, F. A., 179
TYLER, L., 31

W

WECHSLER, H., 123, 140
WEINMAN, B. S., 139, 153
WEISS, R. S., 16
WILDER, J. F., 118
WILENSKY, H. L., 14, 16, 17
WILMER, H. A., 15
WILSON, S., 153
WOLKON, G. H., 141
WRIGHT, G. N., 89

Z

ZUSMAN, J., 138

Subject Index

Subject Index

Denial, 10–12
Directiveness, 37, 38
Disadvantaged, socially and culturally, 52, 110–113, 179, 180
DVR, 79–81, 84, 85, 95

E

Efficacy, 161, 162
Ego, intact or healthy, 2, 29, 177, 178
Ego-involving jobs, 17, 20, 27
Ego strength, 2, 3, 4, 29, 37, 179; and ability to be independent, 2, 3; and regression, 23
El Camino House, 119–122, 128, 129
Emotional capacity. See Ego strength
Enablers, 152–155
Essential concepts, 1–27
Evaluation of rehabilitation programs, 156–176; controlled studies for, 158–161, 163, 164, 165, 169–175; creaming in, 162; efficacy of, 161, 162; employment as criterion for success in, 164; and exposure to multiple programs, 164, 165; and hospital return rates, 163, 164; involving staff, 167, 168; need for, 157, 158, 180; need for administrative support of, 157; negative results of, 169–173; outcome of, 163; process in, 163; quality of, 163; and rapid action research, 167, 168; table of random numbers vs. rotation in, 159; utilization of findings of, 167–169, 173–175
Exconvicts, 179

F

Fairweather's Sheltered Subsociety, 5, 6, 106–110, 174, 175
Family care homes, 6, 7, 115, 122–125, 130
Foreman. See Workshop foreman
Fort Logan Community Mental Health Center, 131

Fountain House, 94, 96–99, 101, 102, 128; group placement program in, 101, 102; satellite housing program in, 128; transitional employment program in, 96–99

G

Gheel Colony, 115
Goodwill Industries, 73, 74, 81, 87
Group placement. See Crew placement
Groups, small problem-solving, 107–109, 174
Guarantor of last resort, 89
Guilt, 25, 26

H

Halfway houses, 4, 115–127, 131–135; for alcoholics, 127, 128; as alternative to hospitalization, 125, 126; in combination with satellite housing, 131, 134, 135; common functions of, 116; community opposition to, 133, 134; as distinguished from boarding homes, 123, 124; as distinguished from hospital, 126; high expectations of residents in, 118–120; length of stay in, 116, 117; life habit training in, 120; for mothers and children, 126, 127; purpose of, 116, 123, 124; shortage of, 133, 134; vocational assistance in, 121, 122; and weekly house meetings, 120
Handcraft Industries, 85
Hero illness, 24
High expectations, 3, 4, 8, 11, 26, 36, 118–120, 129, 130, 137, 138, 142, 144, 145, 148, 149, 178; with flexibility, 4, 144, 148, 178
Horizon House, 144–148
Housing, therapeutic, 114–135

201

Subject Index

I

Indigenous community members, 153, 154

Individual placement, 95–105; of chronic psychiatric patients, 99–101

Inept persons, 12, 13

Instant happiness, 26, 27

Institutionalization, 15, 138, 179

Iowa, University of, 110

J

Jewish Vocational Service of Chicago, 72, 73, 83

Jewish Vocational Service of Los Angeles, 85

Jigs, 76

Job enrichment, 18, 19, 21

Joint Commission on Mental Illness and Health, 115

L

Labeling, 8–13, 141, 142, 178

Leisure, 21, 22

Life habit training, 120, 177

Lounge program, 149, 150

Low expectation settings, 6, 7, 124

M

Manhattan Project, 126

Marginal person in community, 5–8

Menlo Park Veterans' Administration Program, 96, 105, 106

Mental Health Recovery, Inc., 126, 128

N

National Alliance of Businessmen, 110

National Mental Health Act in England, 133

Negative findings, 169–173

Neighborhood Opportunity Centers, 111

Nonverbal responses, 34, 35

Normalization, 10–12

O

Occupational guide, 42, 49

Occupations, 41, 42

On-the-job training, 95

Openness, 39

Optimism, therapeutic, 30, 31

Overhelp, 26

Owens-Illinois Corporation, 110–113

P

Pedregal House, 126, 128

Perkins School for the Blind, 71

Philadelphia Enabler Program, 152–155

Phoenix Houses, 126

Placement, 43, 45, 46, 59, 187; of crew (group), 95, 96, 101, 102, 106–110; of individual, 95–105

Play therapy, 139

President's Commission on National Goals, 20

Prized self-image, 14, 17

Q

Quality control, 183

Quarterway houses, 127

R

Random assignment, 159

Rapid action research, 167, 168

Rationalization of dependency needs, 23, 25

Reality House East, 126

Reality House West, 126

Regression, 22–25

Rehabilitation: coordination of, 1; of exconvicts, 179, 180; involving industry, 97–105, 110–113; in mental hospitals, 1, 2; overly enthusiastic efforts in, 5; of socially and culturally disadvantaged, 52, 110–113, 179, 180

Rehabilitation counseling, 28–49; and chronic patient, 45, 48; confrontation in, 37; and coun-